TAT TVAM ASI
(That Thou Art)

Raphael
(Āśram Vidyā Order)

TAT TVAM ASI

(THAT THOU ART)

The Path of Fire
According to Asparśa-yoga

MOTILAL BANARSIDASS
PUBLISHERS PRIVATE LIMITED • DELHI

First Edition: 1992

Original Title: *Tat tvam asi* (*Tu sei Quello*)
Translated from the Italian by Kay McCarthy

ISBN:81-208-0934-3

Also available at:
MOTILAL BANARSIDASS
41 U.A., Bungalow Road, Jawahar Nagar, Delhi 110 007
120 Royapettah High Road, Mylapore, Madras 600 004
16 St. Mark's Road, Bangalore 560 001
Ashok Rajpath, Patna 800 004
Chowk, Varanasi 221 001

PRINTED IN INDIA
BY JAINENDRA PRAKASH JAIN AT SHRI JAINENDRA PRESS, A-45 NARAINA INDUSTRIAL AREA, PHASE I, NEW DELHI 110 028 AND PUBLISHED BY NARENDRA PRAKASH JAIN FOR MOTILAL BANARSIDASS PUBLISHERS PVT. LTD., BUNGALOW ROAD, JAWAHAR NAGAR, DELHI 110 007

This supreme Brahman, Universal ātman, immense dwelling of all that exists, subtler than any subtle thing and constant: in truth it is yourself, because "That thou art".

(*Kaivalya Upaniṣad*: I, 16)

FOREWORD

The universe is life at multiple dimensions, at multiple systems of coordinates and, by its nature, the individual is the sum or the synthesis of these various systems.

Man is not merely a corporeal and functional complex; he is thought and also spirit, however vague and wornout this term may be.

Science itself has recognized the fact that the universe has more than just one dimension; and it is also becoming evident that the individual has 'faculties' that go beyond the simply corporeal. On the other hand, to think of the human being as a simple function, as a mere glandular secretion and excretion seems to us to be stretching a point too far. To place being exclusively and one-sidedly on his horizontal condition of operativity, seems depriving him of his wholeness, confining his consciousness and intelligence to one sole system of coordinates.

Generally speaking, the Western man has looked outwardly having directed his attention outside of himself in the attempt to conquer the objective nature around himself. There is nothing wrong with this in itself; but it would be wise, indeed necessary, for him to look within himself too, and understand himself in a better way, not limiting his cognitive effort to glands, molecules and tissues but extending it to something more profound. Undoubtedly one should change the direction and the method of investigation; but for the lovers of truth or knowledge obstacles are not so much an impediment as a spur, as is the case with obstacles concerning the objective order of things.

The *yogic*, and at the same time scientific, East has looked within itself and striven to dominate not the nature of the elements without but the nature of its inner elements.

We believe that both approaches, methods and directions, if united and synthesized, would truly produce remarkable results. Spirit and matter could co-exist because they would be recognized as polarities springing from and merging into the Unity of Being.

The ultimate Truth lies in the heart of being and looking for it outside means alienating that very same Truth.

This book tells of a psychological crisis, of an ascesis and of a consequent finding oneself again. It is presented in a dialogue form, and a dialogue is the meeting of two hearts; it is an osmosis of waves vibrating with experiences; it is donation of oneself, vitality that stimulates growth.

A dialogue for its own sake is no real dialogue but only an emotional outburst, a flow of words or a show of erudition.

In a true dialogue there is no competition, no desire, no discharge of tension.

This realizative dialogue between Raphael and Antonio took place over a period of several years and has been adapted to suit the book form. In reality it consisted of intervals, of simple considerations, of long speeches on Antonio's part, and of silence on Raphael's. However, both of the protagonists had two basic aims in common: to seek and find, and to search within themselves.

It is necessary to point out that this book does not ha a scholarly character. Even though the dialogue touches on a number of points of *vedāntic* philosophy, it aims simply at expressing the Doctrine upon which realization is to be based. There is some mention of this fact along the book.

On the other hand, Antonio's way of thinking and the specific *Vedānta* Doctrine required a number of deep discussions concerning metaphysical principles; although the thematic extended much more, we thought to put together that part of it that may be of greater and more direct interest to the Western reader.

Our wish to those who read this book is to seek and find fulfilment within themselves, so that they may also give it to others, if receptive.

Edizioni Āśram Vidyā

CONTENTS

	Foreword	vii
1.	Sensory Life is Conflict	1
2.	What is Intended by Reality	9
3.	Advaita Vedānta	17
4.	Śaṃkara	21
5.	Triple Knowledge	27
6.	Asparśa Yoga	31
7.	Saguṇa Brahman	35
8.	Māyā: Apparent Movement	41
9.	Evolutionism	51
10.	Unity of Tradition	55
11.	Bodily Death	65
12.	Harmony	71
13.	The Qualifications of the Disciple	75
14.	Jung and Western Extroversion	79
15.	Sādhanā	81
16.	The Origin of the Subconsciousness	85
17.	Transmigration	95
18.	Compensations of the Ego	99
19.	Dying to Oneself	105
20.	Being in the World But Not of the World	111
	Index	121

1

SENSORY LIFE IS CONFLICT

A.[1] I am weighed down by doubts, conflict and a distaste for life. I have experienced what we normally call the worldly pleasures, I have devoted myself to painting, I have taken active part in an extremist political current; in other words, I have tried everything, and yet here I am oppressed by a disgust for everything, by restlessness and insecurity. I must also add that I have taken drugs several times. This has debased me even more: I believe I have become addicted to them. How squalid! I am trapped within a vicious circle and I do not know how to escape; I cannot possibly go on like this. If I indulge in experiences without reflecting I feel dulled, alienated, lost; if, on the contrary, I reject experience I am possessed by a terror of loneliness and emptiness. If I am left to myself I am overcome by fear and therefore I look for the company of others; but this makes me feel even emptier than before.

R. My dear one, we can assume two attitudes towards relativistic sensorial experiences. In the first one we identify so deeply with the object of experience that we forget our very being; in this state we feel, as you say, overwhelmed and dulled; rather than experiencing, *we are* experienced, rather than living, we are lived: it is the condition of the animal. In the second we are discerning subjects who discriminate, question themselves and things; but to an investigating and questioning consciousness many experiences may appear absurd, irrational, conflictual. On the other hand, if you question yourself consciously you realize that a sensorial experience appears attractive because *momentarily* you are following the line of least resistance. A thing pleases you because you desire it, but if desire ceases so too does pleasure. And desire, we know, is irrational, capricious and often casts the individual adrift.

---

1. A. = Antonio; R. = Raphael.

A. What shall I do then? Kill myself? I have often thought of doing so, but I have always put it off.

R. Well said. This is merely another desire and desire is not resolved by its gratification, which is just a discharge of tension, but when it is understood and transcended as a result. Have you ever looked desire straight in the face without the support of mental structures?

A. No, I do not understand. The trouble is that I have so many years left ahead of me and this causes me to panic. Why can I not find a solution to my problems? Why is this world so false, so unwilling to engage in a dialogue? I must admit I am really at the end of my tether; I feel that I have almost no strength or perceptive capacity left.

Can you help me? Can you give back to me the dignity of being a man with a mind? I sincerely wished that from these conversations, from our realizative dialogue, as you call it, the certainty of my deeper reality could emerge. In all honesty I believe that this reality is the only anchor of salvation I have been left with.

R. Let me first clarify a number of fundamental points concerning our relationship.

Every true dialogue takes place not between two individuals, but between two hearts, two open consciousnesses, two receptive minds, two pairs of eyes that are all out to understand each other. Wherever there is opposition, reaction, fanaticism and pride there can be no dialogue and no comprehension. To render one's consciousness available does not mean assuming a passive or inert position. To dialogue, in the traditional sense, means to follow a road, a pathway; it means meeting.

A further point is this: the truth of things lies in the things themselves, just as the solution to a problem lies in understanding the problem itself; the truth about being lies within being and to look for it elsewhere is like looking someplace for the very clothes you are wearing.

Again, if the truth that emerges from our dialogue is not *lived* by your consciousness, you will not be able to solve your problems of conflict.

A. I am willing to try anything to find myself; and if I am here it means that there must still be a ray of hope. But I feel it to be so thin!

R. You hope to have the possibility, or rather, the certainty of finding your Reality, is that not so? Well then, it would be advisable first of all to decide upon what we mean by the word Reality.

What do you intend by Reality? What meaning has this word for you?

A. For me real is whatever I can experience, perceive, observe, whatever falls under my sensorial awareness.

R. And yet, up to now, the 'reality' that you have experienced has caused you only conflict, confusion and uncertainty; on the other hand it is precisely for this reason that you wish to turn towards other realities. Is that not so?

A. Yes, it is.

R. How many realities are there for you then?

A. I would venture to say that there are multiple experiences of the one Reality.

R. In that case, being part of a sole Reality, experiences should be considered as being just as real; now, if the experiences you have had and which you consider a part of Reality have only brought you conflict, you must reasonably suppose that also other possible realities can only bring you unfulfilment.

A. Do not lead me into a blind alley, I beg of you! I am already trapped. Am I destined to live in this state of conflict and uncertainty forever? Is this my destiny? And why me?

R. My dear one, you must relax. I tell you that if you are here there is still a chance; and in fact you have understood that yourself.

You see, if you have come here merely to be comforted, I can even give you comfort, but I assure you that the real problems of life are not solved by begging for pity. I am sure that if you put yourself into a proper position of consciousness, you will slowly find yourself.

A. What makes you believe that?

R. Your intelligence and your sufferings which have brought to maturation your consciousness.

A. Do you trust me? Can you trust a failure like me? A degraded drug addict who has also hated?

R. Yes. Otherwise I should have not accepted you. My dear one, you have accepted me and I have accepted you, and there is nothing more beautiful than accepting each other, than meeting. Do you not agree?

A. You make me feel ashamed. I am here out of despair. It is not I but my despair that accepts you; can you see how sad this fact is? But you, why do you accept me?

R. It is not I but my bliss and my understanding that accept you.

A. Why does your 'I' not accept me? Did you not say that meeting is a beautiful thing?

R. It does not accept you for the simple fact that the understanding and bliss I have spoken of are devoid of ego.

A. What strange words you speak!

R. However, we have gone a little too far ahead. Later on you will understand what I mean. We were saying...?

A. I was asking you whether I am destined to go on living forever in this state of perpetual conflict and uncertainty.

R. I cannot give you an answer; we have to look for a way out together.

You say that even though you have had 'real' experiences in so many fields of the human expression, you feel totally empty, unhappy, in conflict and on the brink of despair, is that not so?

A. Yes, that is right, I do not deny it.

R. Now then, if all you have experienced truly belonged to the order of the reality, do you think you would have arrived at this degree of confusion?

A. What do you mean? Should reality bring happiness and rejoicing?

R. You said before that you would like to find the certainty of your inmost Reality at last. I suppose that this yearning for realization is due to the fact that, hoping to find the Reality of yourself, you at the same time hope to find the bliss of your heart; otherwise why go on experiencing more realities-illusions? Am I wrong?

A. That is exactly so. I would like to emerge from this state of solitude and restlessness. I already said that I would like to find my innermost Reality because I think that only through it will I be able to find myself in peace.

R. Therefore, only your true Reality can give you the certainty of total fulfilment. This implies, we may say, that all those other external realities, although perceived and experienced, were unable to give you fulfilment. This leads us to conclude that they are not realities after all and that, most likely, what you have perceived and experienced must have belonged to a certain order of enslaving phenomena. Sensory perception is not synonymous with Reality.

A. However, I must add that I have known moments of happiness and enjoyment. Drugs have enslaved me but they have also given me, and they still do, instants of happiness and well-being.

R. You said *moments*, even *instants*, which implies that the particular event-thing giving you happiness and well-being did not belong to an absolute reality but to a relative, contingent truth. Now, do you want fleeting, discontinuous happiness that comes and goes, or do you want *to be* constant bliss?

On the other hand, if this happiness-enjoyment of moments

and instances, however much experienced, has forced you into solitude and uncertainty, we must deduce that it does not lead to total fulfilment. Do you not agree?

If your perception-sensations and the experiences that you have had up to now had given you fulfilment, do you think that you would find yourself in the conditions you are in today?

A. I do not think so. I would have had no reason for being here and in these conditions. But is there not the chance that psychologically I am a misfit therefore finding it very hard to harmonize with life?

R. I do not think so because, all told, you have experienced every formula offered by life, you have plunged into every kind of activity and relations, you have had ideals, you have communicated, only that all this has left you unsatisfied; it has not *filled* you, it has not given you what you had hoped. You have to admit that there may be consciousnesses to which this kind of relational life is no longer suited. If you wished to live in the jungle sharing the way of life of the 'bushman', you would obviously feel yourself unsuited, but this is not indicative of any kind of psychic flaw in yourself, quite the contrary.

We may conclude that some consciousnesses are prepared to assimilate expressions of another order of reality.

A. This consoles me, but how can I understand that, let us say so, my case is one of consciousness growth and not one of mere escape?

R. It is very simple. When there is only psychic unbalance there always remains, in the consciousness background, an unfulfilled desire to experience, a wish to express oneself according to that particular expression of life. In other words, one *would like to* but cannot because there are psychic resistances or impediments. Therefore, a part of us requests while the other, for various reasons, is unable to open itself up to experience. In this case, all that is necessary to do is to re-educate the impeded part and everything goes back into its proper place.

A. But I have experienced, lived, suffered and sometimes even known joy; only that this kind of life-style has in no way solved my basic problems.

R. Which means that this world made up of acquisitions, of sensory appetites of all kinds and degrees, this society based upon profit, consumerism, competition, violence and drugs, this world which is trying to achieve freedom *of* the ego rather than freedom *from* the ego, has not found in you a consciential response, it has not given you that kind of fulfilment your soul is looking for. Your endless frustrations, anxieties, your refusal and your uncertainty depend on this. Today's society has confined itself exclusively into a physical world, but the being, in its entirety, is something more than a physical body with its glandular secretions.

A. You are right. Sufferings and conflict are not always the outcome of psychological immaturity, quite the opposite. Pain is manysided but often—convinced as we are that it has just one direction-motive—we make it impossible for ourselves to understand it properly. On the other hand, in order to grasp the meaning of this event we should know of the existence of other directions. What is lacking in this one-sided, one-way society of ours is the recognition that the Individual is more than the individual, that Man in his wholeness is something more than his condition as man. The individual in this petrified society has forced himself into limits that suffocate and mortify him.

You have spoken about assimilating an expression of *reality* of a different order. In fact I realize that we should agree upon the meaning of the term 'reality' so that I can understand all the implications.

2

WHAT IS INTENDED BY REALITY

R. This is the first time I hear you speak like a true *homo sapiens.* Very well, let us get back to the heart of the matter. What do we intend by Reality? What meaning do we ascribe to this word?

A. At this point you must illumine me as to why I am unable to penetrate the essence of certain things. I am rooted in the conviction that everything I see and experience must be real. It seems so natural that I should think this way.

R. Let us try to understand one another. In conclusion, for reality you mean what you can perceive, experience, what your senses can catch, and so on. On the other hand I agree that the common idea of reality is the one you have. But we should see whether this concept is true or not, do you agree?

Our thesis therefore is this: what do we mean by reality? Through which means or instruments can we achieve it? What is the outcome of the knowledge of reality?

Empirical realism holds that every given element that can be examined by our perceptive organs is real and therefore the 'becoming-movement' is real.

A. So I am right. Did not I say precisely this?

R. Yes, this is what you said, but realism also holds that there are things which, although perceived sensorially, and therefore experienced, are not real.

A. This amazes me. How can one experience non-real data? What we are saying sounds like a contradiction to me, a nonsense.

R. A mirage in the desert, although positively perceived, is not real. We may see two moons, but we are told that one is real while the second is false, because it belongs to the phenomenon of refraction. We hear a sound which others do not; now this sound, for empirical realism is not real because it cannot be perceived by other people as it is, in fact, a subjective datum. We perceive a static form like that of a stone, but we are told that this form is not really static but dynamic, because it is made up of an electronic mass in continuous movement. How many things have you perceived under the influence of drugs that later proved not to be true at all? As you can see not all the things that your senses perceive are true or correct. We said before that perception is not synonymous with Reality.

A. This is the first time I awake to such an awareness.

R. Certainly, the majority of people is, as it were, asleep without even knowing it. And if you stop taking drugs you will acquire even greater awareness, although drugs may create the illusion of a greater psychic lucidity and vitality. In any case, all this leads us to conclude that there is a contradiction in the formulation of reality, and a contradictory reality is not absolute reality. Do you agree?

A. Of course. Do you know something? I am beginning to like philosophy.

R. Very well; man differentiates from animals because of the use of reason. Even empirical realism itself recognizes the insufficiency of the perceptive organs, and in order to give an event-thing the patent of validity it has made use of the method of investigation based upon the reproducibility of the experiments (the repetition of the observation-experiment) and on the requirement that others (besides ourselves) be able to perceive the experiment-observation and repeat it at will. This method of investigation, however, presents a number of flaws and is unable to withstand a careful analysis.

A. I have always believed that this method was infallible, therefore it is difficult for me to see any error of judgment in it. The object which proves to be stable and constant, and the universality of consensus concerning it are certainly sufficient elements for maintaining its reality.

R. I beg you to clear your mind of preconceptions and to concentrate upon what we are saying.

The repetition of the observation-experiment presupposes the conviction that a datum, in order to be real, must always exist; that is, it must be *constant* in time. It must, every time we observe or experience it, be in that same state of being, intrinsic to its nature. The characteristic of being real refers to the temporal condition, to the duration.

If, for example, the sun rises on the horizon and this occurs constantly, then we may *suppose* that this event is real. Here lies the flaw. We know that every empirical thing undergoes a process of modification, transformation and disintegration or disappearance. Today we may observe a datum, and tomorrow we may no longer be able to do so. This means that the time 'constant' does not represent the constant after all. Science tells us that a star is born, grows and vanishes; it follows that the temporal condition cannot be held to be real and therefore we have to admit the fact that the method of reproducibility of the event is not of an absolute but only of a relative kind. Time itself is merely an element of perception.

A. However, we have also to admit that if a given fact is observed several times it must exist. We cannot perceive nothing; the eyes, and the other senses, cannot see nothingness.

R. That is right. What this something is we shall see later on. For the time being we are interested in isolating the concept of reality.

Another flaw in the empirical argument is when we say that an event, in order to be proved, must be reproduced or seen by other people. So, not only must sunrise be seen *continuously* by us who affirm the fact, but it must also be seen by other people because its affirmation must possess the character of universality.

A. This seems right to me, otherwise anyone might declare seeing things that do not in reality exist.

R. We are forgetting to keep some very important things in mind, however.

A. But the affirmation of a fact shared by many seems to me to be true beyond any doubt.

R. When we affirm the existence of a given fact we may ask ourselves: are all the observing subjects on the same particular system of co-ordinates as our own? If this is so we have to accept that the observation-event refers only to that particular set of co-ordinates and not to any other. This implies that we are speaking about a general, and not universal, affirmation. The general falls within the sphere of the individual, it is the individual generalized. So, the case might be given that an individual who is located on a different set of co-ordinates—let us imagine an individual living outside of the earth's orbit—does not perceive what we do. In fact, living outside of our time-space dimension, he could perceive neither sunrise nor sunset. And if we were to speak to him of dawn and sunset, of daylight and darkness, he would surely think we were talking nonsense. In other words, for him the dawn-event would be a non-reality, while for us it is undeniably true.

There is a further consideration to be made: do all the other observers have the same cognitive means as we do? If they do, then they cannot but see what we see. If we all have eyes made in such a way as to perceive tridimensional data, we can see no more than tridimensional data. Here too there is a problem of limitation, so that we can say that the reality observed concerns those observers who are equipped with the same cognitive instruments and are on the same set of time-space coordinates. All told, it is a *relative* and not an absolute reality.

We can draw some conclusions from what we have been saying: for the empirical realism, reality is all we perceive in an objective way, but this reality is not absolute because there are things that we perceive and which are not real. Upon what is the proof of the reality or not of a given fact based? The answer is: upon a particular method of investigation which consists of the repeated and continuous observation of the event-framework and in the requirement that said event-framework may be observed and experienced at will by others. When we have the recurrence of the event-observation and the generalized possibility of verifying it, then the fact is said to be real. But this type of reality is of a sensory-analytical order, therefore fruit of infra-individual knowledge, of knowledge referred to the five senses and co-ordinated by the empirical, selective mind, a mind belonging to a particular *order of consciousness*; we can say in scientific terms: to a particular and well-defined consciential-mental set of co-ordinates. Besides, we have seen that such reality is not absolute but relative, therefore contradictory.

On the other hand, cognitive realism or empirical knowledge was thoroughly analysed by the philosopher Immanuel Kant who demonstrated that it does not correspond at all to *reality in itself*, but to a simple mental representation of it which we are able to produce. Therefore, by means of empirical knowledge we cannot grasp the *reality*–tree in its intrinsic identity but only our mental representation of it, which is quite a different matter.

Another very important aspect of this kind of relativist knowledge is that it aims at acquiring notions about the quantity of things without bringing the individual any qualitative consciential improvement. It is not, therefore, transforming, cathartic, creative knowledge, but one which is directed merely along a horizontal line of experimentation.

If you now consider all these things you will be able to understand that your indefinite movements along the horizontal line have only brought you to multiply your sensorial experiences and relations without transforming and improving your consciousness; they have, on the contrary, caused the degradation of your very soul. Thus, you have an erudition of facts, events, relations concerning the different aspects of life, but peace is still missing from your heart.

However, we must recognize the fact that the fundamental aspiration of scientific empiricism itself is that of finding a *constant*, a universally valid, a permanent identity in all things. This is, in fact, what Max Planck says in his *Scientific Autobiography:* "In the first paragraph of this autobiographical scheme

I underlined the fact that for me the research of something absolute is the noblest and highest aim of science. The reader might hold this to be in contradiction with my declared interest in the theory of relativity. But it would be fundamentally wrong to look at things this way, as all that is relative presupposes the existence of something absolute. The common expression 'all is relative' is ambiguous and senseless. Even the theory of relativity is based on something absolute, that is the metric measurement of the time-space continuum; and the research for the absolute, which alone can give meaning to relative things, is a particular interesting task.... It is our task to find in all these factors and data the absolute, the universally valid, the invariable which is hidden in them."

The task of every sincere and authentic researcher is therefore that of finding the *constant*, the universally valid, the invariable and the oneness of that constant. This means finding that which really *is*, not what appears to be; and nothing but Being in the proper sense of the word is that which really *is*.

We have arrived at our basic problem: the individual is anxiously looking for Being, for what he really is, for the Real in its universal, and not its general, sense, for Truth in its total Oneness, and not in its fragmented and contradictory aspects. Every true philosopher, scientist, believer, every authentic researcher is doing simply this: looking for the Constant, for the Absolute Reality.

* * *

A. Here I am to take up our dialogue again. In this past period of time my mind has been absorbed by what you have said to me and therefore I have had no time to think about my woes or go out with my friends. What a strange thing to find myself suddenly plunged into a world of thought and of philosophical problems!

R. My dear one, I am trying to pull you off the shoals and help you to find an island where you can find protection from the torpid experiences of your past; from there you can take flight for other shores on your own wings.

A. Do you think that I shall be able to make it?

R. I told you that I have faith in your intelligence.

A. I feel reassured, besides the fact that I am happy to know that someone is trusting me.

So, if I have understood properly, we should give the concept of Reality the attributes of constant, universally valid and invariable.

R. Let us say that Reality as such has no attributes; those particular aspects concerning the constant, etc., are consubstantial with Reality itself. When we say that the individual is life, the term 'life' is not an attribute of the individual but consubstantial to the individual himself; an individual devoid of life cannot exist, and life not manifesting itself through an expressing consciousness cannot be called life.

A. I have perfectly understood that Reality is constant, invariable, universal, and from this I deduce that I must find this constant within myself.

R. I see that you are opening up to intuition. At this point I think that true help can come to you from a philosophy that can actually indicate this constant to you.

If in you there really is a thirst for Reality-constant, then you have to discover the right Doctrine that can lead you on to the path of the infinite and universal Being. Do you not think so?

A. Of course, and I agree with you. I feel lighter, more certain and happier. I have come to a wonderful conclusion: there is a constant Reality because I believe, like Planck, that the usual phrase 'all is relative' is meaningless; my incompleteness tells me that my wholeness must also exist; behind the veil of my conflict-suffering there must be endless joy, behind the hallucinations of drugs I take there must be something real.

At this point I would like to know Reality as meant by *Advaita Vedānta* and *Asparśa-yoga* of which you are a knower. On the other hand, this is the reason why I am here.

3

ADVAITA VEDĀNTA

R. Well then, I shall give you some explanations according to my understanding and my own experience.

For *Advaita* Reality must be constant, identical to itself, self-evident, indivisible, infinite, beyond time, space and causality.

If absolute Reality were to change or depend upon other realities or to be conditioned by time-space-causality, or still, if it were of an inconstant and contradictory order it would not be absolute Reality. A reality which we can perceive today but no longer perceive tomorrow, cannot be considered as absolute Reality.

A reality which is born, grows and then vanishes cannot be considered as being beyond time-space-causality; a divided and fragmentary reality is not Reality, because in this case a contradiction would be introduced upon the plane of the Principle-reality which would annul the Principle itself.

We should remember that when *Advaita* speaks of the constant, this term must be taken in its purest acceptation; the constant is what is permanent, it is what *is,* because if it were to undergo even the slightest interruption, a change or a becoming, then it would not be constant.

The constant—by the way—besides being an axiom or self-evident fact, is logically inferable from certain effects we can see. Planck, we have seen, and you have recalled this yourself, rightly states that the phrase 'all is relative' is ambiguous and meaningless, as what is relative presupposes the existence of an absolute, adding—and this is very important—that the relative can have a meaning *only* when compared to something absolute.

Another characteristics of Reality for *Advaita*, is that it must be self-evident, non-contradictory and universal.

Self-evidence is fundamental because a reality that is not founded upon itself cannot be called Reality; a reality which must look for support in other truths of the same or of another order cannot be called Reality.

Any contradiction arising from Reality would lead to the annulment of the Real itself. A reality that contradicts itself is no Reality.

Universality is another aspect consubstantial to the Reality-Constant. Let us remember that universal does not mean general. The general is merely the individual generalized, while the universal implies unity and totality, apart from any individual or particular aspect. We shall see that *Advaita Vedānta* carries out the scrutiny of Reality taking into consideration all systems of co-ordinates.

A Reality, being of a universal order, must be valid upon all possible systems of co-ordinates: within time and beyond it, on our own plane as well as on the numberless planes of manifestation. If a reality is so for us and not for a hypothetical inhabitant of Sirius, it means that such a reality is not universal but peculiar to specific existential plane.

If a reality is such for us but not for a *Deva* (Angel) or for the Divinity itself, then it cannot be considered universal. Thus, for *Advaita* Reality must be constant, universal, self-evident and non-contradictory.

As you can see, with *Advaita* we are before a rigorous analysis of the concept of Reality, an analysis which aims at avoiding all approximation and misunderstanding.

Seeing that the empirical realism is unable to give a true concept of the Constant and universal, we should keep in mind that the Infinite of the *Advaita* is not the mathematical infinite of empirical realism, the One of the *Advaita* is not the mathematical one of empirical realism: the mathematical one already implies the many because it is, indeed, quantity.

We shall speak later on about the type of knowledge *Advaita* avails of in order to comprehend the Constant.

A. I intend to reflect and meditate on all this because I find it truly interesting. A new vision of knowing and approaching things is slowly making its way into my consciousness. I was on a plane of action-identification without even having the time to reflect, or to think by synthesis. I understand that Man is gifted with a treasure within himself that he is usually unable to appreciate.

The most difficult thing is to find someone capable of guiding you to reason in terms of universality, of unity and of synthesis; of enabling you to reason, very simply stated. So far, I have always come across people who have just urged me to act, to have experiences in the sphere of the infra-sensory perception, therefore I could not but be in a vicious circle.

The majority of mankind moves along a one-dimensional, one-sided line, finding itself periodically in a state of crisis because the line, returning and closing upon itself, offers no escape route. It is the condition of a snake biting its own tail.

R. Right, I appreciate this image. Quite a few individuals carry on and experience, let us say, *happily* in the infra-sensorial dimension, because that line has not yet closed in upon itself, but sooner or later it will. A person travelling straight around the globe, sooner or later will arrive back to where he started; the ring will inevitably close, as it did in your case. The same will occur to all those following this horizontal line of unfulfilment.

A. I am immensely happy to change direction, even though many other doubts are likely to crop up. What a strange feeling! I have just remembered something and I would like to tell you about it. For some time I have been led to believe that truth can be made up, can be invented: that Man creates his own truth-reality and that whoever is best able at it may even impose 'his' truth on others.

R. It is true; this is the common opinion, especially in certain circles. If we want to reason wisely, how can we accept such a statement? The individual can always formulate theories and make categorical statements, but we must admit that if these ideas and statements do not correspond to the universally true and just, to what a thing really *is,* sooner or later they cannot but collapse and die. On the other hand it has always been that way in history. Theories and truths wrought by the individual pride, self-assertion and vanity have come to life, have lived even for centuries but they have also been brushed away by the power of the emerging Reality, consumed by the fire of a newly awakened consciousness of mass, or of beings who have revealed the truth as purely such. The history of mankind is for the most part the story of crime, infamy, authoritarian statement, demagogy at all levels and prevarication; and all this because it is the history of false values, false doctrines, false truths.

* * *

A. In these past days I have meditated upon what we talked about and I see how valid our dialogue is. Although I am still conditioned by my empirical mind, I shall do my best to be open.

I have studied *Advaita* in part, but I still have numerous doubts. I shall try to express them. For example, I would like to know whether *Advaita* is theistic.

R. For *Advaita* theism belongs to a particular level of truth. Non-dualism admits the principle of *Īśvara* or *saguṇa Brahman* as the principial, qualified Entity, that is an Entity with attributes.

A. From this point of view can we say that *Advaita Vedānta* is a religion?

R. From this standpoint we can consider it as expressing a religious spirit. It is not, however, religion in the Western sense of the word.

The approach to *saguṇa Brahman* is effected in a ritual-devotional, emotional spirit. This implies that religious ritualism, ethics, faith and all that regards the realm of the relationship between God and the created being are accepted by *Advaita Vedānta*, though within the limits relevant to certain consciential levels.

4

ŚAṂKARA

A. Why, then, did Śaṃkara oppose the religious ritualism of his own caste?

R. Śaṃkara did not fight against ritual as such and religion, it was actually he who rearranged the various religious organizations, reorganized the *svāmi* orders, etc. Besides he also professed his *Śivaite* religion and it is therefore a mistake to believe that Śaṃkara fought against the ritualistic religion of the Fathers and all it involved. Instead, he made the *brāhmaṇa* ritualists understand the relativity of their doctrine. The brahmin order had actually become crystallized around certain formal aspects of the One-Reality, ignoring the deeper spirit of that same unqualified Reality. By presenting the *Advaita*, the principle of Non-duality, Śaṃkara reproposed and pointed out the supreme a-formal Reality. We may say that, rather than fighting against and oppose religion, Śaṃkara went beyond the religion of the Fathers.

In the *Śruti*, upon which religion itself is founded, one finds two aspects of truth of the one Reality (*parā and aparā*); they represent the unqualified, absolute *nirguṇa Brahman* bereft of attributes, and *saguṇa Brahman*, the God-Person with attributes. Now, the priestly order had remained anchored to the concept of the God-Person, often disregarding and even denying the unqualified, attributeless supreme Reality or *nirguṇa*. In other words, the priestly caste followed the 'Lesser Mysteries', wrongly considering them as absolute, while Śaṃkara re-established the 'Great Mysteries' upon which the former depend.

The difficulty he had to face was enormous because the minds of the priests and of the people, which followed that *Vedic* ritual religion, were unable to grasp the deeper and more elevated truth which Śaṃkara tried, through the *Śruti*, to demonstrate.

A. What does the *Śruti* say about this?

R. The *Śruti* (*Vedas* and *Upaniṣads*) plainly speaks about a Being which is One-and-without-a-second (and Śaṃkara's quotations about this point are numerous) and at the same time about a Being which is the Lord of the manifest worlds (*Puruṣa, Īśvara, Rudra*, etc.)

Śaṃkara underlines the fact that there are two orders of truth: the one based on the subject-object interaction and therefore empirical, conceptual and dual, the other absolute, impersonal, a-formal and supreme. In other words, a *saguṇa* truth (*aparā vidyā*) and a *nirguṇa* one (*parā vidyā*).

A. Therefore Śaṃkara introduced a dualism.

R. Not at all. He argued that there is only one Reality, and that this Reality, just to give it a name, is called *Brahman*. The empirical truth (*Brahmā*) is but a mere reflection of this Reality. And indeed, compared with the sole Reality, empirical reality is simply a mental representation, a verbal concept and nothing more.

A. Is this what Śaṃkara holds?

R. It is not held by Śaṃkara, but by the very same *Śruti* when it states that empirical reality or *māyā* is only a simple classification or concept of names and forms.

A. How could this concept of *māyā* be expressed in Western terms?

R. The idea that best corresponds to *māyā* is that of phenomenon. "... This duality is merely *māyā* also called phenomenal world" (*Māṇḍūkya Upaniṣad*, Chapter I, *kārikā* 17)

Śaṃkarian *māyā* corresponds, therefore, to what we might call 'movement that shapes and forms', changing phenomenon, while the noumenon corresponds to the concept of the God-Person or of Being (*Brahmā, Īśvara*, etc.). Besides, *māyā*, veiling Reality, makes things appear to be what they are not: therefore, a datum *appears* to us what it is not.

For example, Earth *appears* to us to stand still and yet it is moving. The sun *appears* to be high or low in the sky, but in actual fact it is situated in limitless space and is neither high nor low—these are simple concepts or names of reference. Matter *appears* to be solid, compact and indivisible, and yet it is simply electronic energy that has assumed a given form.

As you can see, many things appear to be what they are not: this is the work of *māyā*.

A. So, Non-dualism is a kind of monism, is it not?

R. If by the term monism is meant divine or principial Unity (Being) from which all emanates, this does not correspond exactly to the concept of *Advaita*.

The One is related to the many, it is the beginning of a series, while the term *Advaita* reflects the idea of Non-duality or of One-without-a-second: this definition is made precisely in order to convey the idea that this Unity has no beginning, no correlation. We can also add that it corresponds to the metaphysical Zero or Non-being. Non-dualism goes beyond monism itself, beyond the very concept of Being. Being is already necessity; Non-being, insofar as it is absolute, is Freedom.

A. But then, if the *Vedic* priesthood do not recognize the supreme Reality, *nirguṇa*, Non-dualism does not recognize empirical reality, *saguṇa*.

R. This is not correct because Non-dualism accepts just the same empirical reality with all it involves, only that it does not consider it as being supreme and absolute Reality. It does not deny the world, nature, or any other expression of life, but it points out the fact that this world, and therefore this level of truth, is not absolute Reality, is not real in itself, is not self-existing.

A. But Śaṃkara requested that the seekers of *Brahman* renounce the world totally and refuse life.

R. In this case, too, it is essential to understand Śaṃkara's standpoint. He revealed that the *nirguṇa Brahman* is the one supreme Reality. Now, if you wished to realize the Absolute, Unqualified Unity, it would seem obvious that you should renounce this world which expresses itself through the relative and empirical truth. If you wish to realize the total and integral Reality, you have to drop half-truths and all those expressions which are only simple formal and nominal aspects. You cannot pursue Truth while remaining in error. But this condition refers exclusively to the *Advaita saṃnyāsin* and does not concern those who are still following religious ritualism.

In the *Vedānta* Tradition, there are four stages of life which correspond to the student, the householder, the hermit and the renouncer. Śaṃkara is not against this tradition, but points out the fact that if one aims at the *nirguṇa* Reality one has to follow a certain path. It all depends on what one's purpose is: if the individual wishes to follow the *nirguṇa* realization, he obviously needs to transcend all those qualitative expressions and those attributes belonging to the 'Lesser Mysteries'. On the other hand, by merging into the One-without-a-second all those antinomies and desires inherent in the empirical world disappear. In other words, the world of *māyā* vanishes.

A. This implies that the *Advaita* realized one by renouncing the world, and therefore the action required by this world, comes to find himself in a condition of mere inert abstraction.

R. The *Advaita* realized one carries out only two actions: the one which concerns the maintenance of his body-projection, as long as this exists, and the other concerning the transformation of the consciousness of those who knock looking for Being. But, all told, for the *Advaitin* these are not real actions or duties but simple, natural, innocent, spontaneous acts, it is a joyous revelation such as the fragrance of a flower.

Thus the *Advaitin* does not represent an abstraction in the phenomenal world, but a reality with its particular expression.

On the other hand, a Reality, as such, cannot constitute an abstraction in the sense of something that is not.... It is of no importance if others do not understand this kind of Reality. Being cannot but be, and if it is, it does not create the problem of doing or not doing, of standing still or moving, of speaking or keeping quiet, of being here or there, above or below, etc.

A. How does Non-dualism consider the non-Hindu religions?

R. Non-dualism has an eminently universal and synthetic conception of life; all differentiation, separation and sectarianism are the outcome of that *avidyā* expressed by the empirical mind. Non-dualism, in its deepest expression, is neither religion nor philosophy as it is understood in the West, nor theology, but pure metaphysics, and a metaphysical vision of life cannot be in opposition with anything or anybody. Metaphysics takes up the standpoint of the Absolute, of the Unity-without-a-second, and therefore regards all conceptual or ideological factors, all psychological manifestations, etc., as simple aspects or degrees of the supreme Truth. It is equally true that all these degrees of truth are annulled in supreme Truth.

A. But by making converts, do you not oppose the other religious organizations?

R. A true *Advaitin* does not make converts because Truth does not need promoters. Non-dualism discloses ultimate Reality which can only be expounded to and lived by those who are ready for it. It is just at a sentimental level that one feels under the urge to make converts, that one feels invested with the *task*, the mission of going all out to transform the others; but *Advaita* does not set itself upon the sentimental plane. Whoever has reached the Centre stays as 'unmoved mover' with special possibilities of influence.

A. Who on earth can ever reach this type of rarefied Realization?

R. Without doubt, *Advaita* is not for the many, not because it is reserved to a privileged minority, but because just a few are truly willing to die to themselves. The majority seek worldly, intellectual, psychic and spiritual *acquisitions*. Besides, its *sādhanā*, based upon the comprehension of the one Being and the absolute Constant, does not find a response within the common man's mind which is used to being lazy and unused to investigating.

A. But we are told to transcend the mind which is an obstacle to the realization of *Brahman*.

5

TRIPLE KNOWLEDGE

R. For *Advaita*, the Realization is attained through Knowledge and Knowledge is reached through questioning, investigating and understanding oneself. We have three types of knowledge:

—that which is the outcome of subject-object relation (empirical knowledge or practical reason, indicative knowledge or knowledge of particulars)

—that which is the effect of supraconscious intuition (synthetic knowledge or pure reason)

—transcendental knowledge, which is the fruit of identity (supreme Knowledge or Knowledge by identity, *Parā Vidyā*).

These three types of learning offer three levels of truth. As the neophyte progresses, he overcomes and abandons a certain cognitive level because this has already served its purpose. The ultimate Reality can be known through a Knowledge *by identity* which leaves out of consideration the first two levels of knowledge. Being knows itself through itself. The ultimate Reality is not known but It is *realized* and disclosed through identity.

A. I would like to go more deeply into this concept because I always thought there was only one way of knowing.

R. This is true, there is one knowledge but the operative modalities are three. Let us clarify this point.

We have before us a cube, a tetrahedral figure and a parallelepiped; as you can see they are made of cardboard and represent three forms-volumes made from the same material-substance, that is the cardboard. Depending on the angle from which we look at them we can have two points of view: one is that which sees *only* the form of the tetrahedral shape, of the cube, etc., the other is that which sees the only substance represented by the cardboard. Whoever sees only the geometrical forms observes from the empirical outlook, while whoever sees the underlying substance observes from an intuitive-synthetic standpoint. The first expresses himself in terms of multiplicity and of quantity, the second in terms of synthesis and unity. They are in any case two ways of looking at things, two attitudes or approaches to Truth. We say intuitive knowledge because the sensible eyes, which see only volumes and shapes, cannot grasp the inner truth expressing the essence-substance unity. Thus, this kind of truth is the fruit of intuition and not of perception-seeing through the senses.

The example of the cardboard is similar to that of the clay and the different forms-jars it can be shaped into. We may see the jars in terms of clay or the clay in terms of jars.

A. Therefore the outcome is the same, both are real.

R. Not quite. If we wish to examine things in depth we have to admit that the cause is more than the effect. This cube-form in front of us is only a 'substantial-consciential moment' of the cardboard which is the only eternal and *constant* factor transcending the form of the cube. The cube form comes and goes but the cardboard remains and survives the disintegration of the cube. This implies that it must belong to different order of reality. The same holds with regard to the jar and the clay. If we wish to take the correct standpoint we must recognize that the jar is merely a relative-moment as compared with the clay-constant; thus too, any golden object-form whatsoever is contingent and fleeting with regard to the substance gold. Hence the two orders of knowledge and the two cognitive aspects (empirical, selective or particular knowledge, and synthetic knowledge).

The error of considering the empirical view absolute leads to this absurd statement: "I see only distinct forms, therefore the ultimate reality consists of forms and quantity".

But this is not all: we can thoroughly study all the indefinite distinct forms adopting the empirical outlook, the study will never be able to attain the synthetic intuitive knowledge (and its order of truth) because the empirical knowledge of a form non-real added to the empirical knowledge of another form non-real can only give two non-realities. A relative added to a relative can only add up to two relatives. There are some politico-philosophical doctrines that state, in absolute terms, that only individuals or corporeal-formal entities exist ignoring their unity-essence; in other words they postulate the object without the subject, the phenomenon without the noumenon.

From this view ensues, as a result, a false concept of life and a false order of values. On this basis one arrives at formulating a distorted truth which results in absolute individualism and unavoidable conflict between these individuals: a power struggle in its precise sense, a distinction between classes and on the basis of colour; a truth which results in a demagogy which consists in taking advantage of the weak points of others. The history of mankind is the story of this struggle for supremacy rather than for transcending themselves.

A. However, we can see the multiplicity or the quantity in the unity and the unity in the quantity-multiplicity.

R. You are right, this truth is the outcome of synthetic and unifying knowledge. All entities are formal aspects made in the 'image' of the Principle, naturally with reference to the *essence* and not to the form-substance; forms vary in quantity and quality. All planes and volumes are made in the image of the point. From this point of view the idea of the One as opposed to the multiple, or the idea of how the One can create multiplicity is improperly posed. The One contains in itself the potentiality of diversity just as the one mind contains in itself the potentiality of manifesting multiple modes of formal and non-formal expression, without however annulling its nature.

A. However, I do not understand what supreme Knowledge, or Knowledge based upon identity, means.

R. Beyond the essence out of which all things are made, exists the very root of essence. Essence is only *one* of the infinite principles of absolute Reality. Beyond the point, as *first cause*, we have the root of the point the reality of which belongs to another order.

So we have the following scheme:

Empirical, selective-particular knowledge Science	Differentiation of forms Manifest entities ↓
Synthetical, principial knowledge	Essence-substance *Puruṣa-Prakṛti* Universal polarities ↓
Philosophy, Ontology	Principial Unity *Īśvaric* Seed *Saguṇa Brahman* ↓
Knowledge by identity Metaphysics	Unqualified Absolute *Nirguṇa Brahman* The Infinite

(Sphere of Māyā: Differentiation of forms … *Saguṇa Brahman*)

Knowledge by identity is metaphysics and, contrary to the first two types of knowledge which are based on the subject-object relationship, it is the outcome of Realization and not of discussion. In conclusion we can say that there is a *sole* Knowledge which has different modes of expression on different planes of investigation.

A. So, *yoga* is not necessary for *Advaita Vedānta*?

6

ASPARŚA YOGA

R. *Advaita* goes beyond the kind of *yoga* which is based upon psycho-physical aspects; there is no *yoga* more elevated than *understanding.*

He whose mind and heart are fused and pointed at *understanding* goes directly to the centre of Being. In any case, if we are allowed the expression, *Advaita* has its own *yoga* which is called *Asparśa-yoga.*

Asparśa means without contact, without relations, without support. It is a *yoga* which is experienced by means of that triple knowledge we have already spoken about. Thus, it is a very particular *yoga.*

Brahman or the Absolute has no supports, because the Absolute rests upon itself alone; being One-without-a-second it cannot have any relation with anything. Therefore, *Asparśa-yoga* is the *yoga* of becoming *nirguṇa Brahman*; it is the *yoga* of Non-duality; it is the *yoga* of the true *saṃnyāsin.*

A. Who invented this *yoga*?

R. This *yoga* was not invented; it is to be found in the *Upaniṣads* but the person who made it known was Gauḍapāda.

Gauḍapāda—under the influence of Nārāyaṇa, the God-principle—revealed this *yoga* to men eagerly looking for Knowledge-realization. He immortalized it in the *kārikā*-verses which he added to the *Māṇḍūkya Upaniṣad* and which, in turn, were commented by the great Teacher Śaṃkara. Thus, this *Upaniṣad* is extremely important for the Non-dualistic *Vedānta,* because the two great interpreters of Non-dualism converge here codifying and co-ordinating what we might call *Advaita-asparśa,* just as Patañjali co-ordinated the classical *Rāja-yoga.* Today this *yoga* is still taught by disciples scattered all over the world and linked together by the 'chain' or the *āśrama* of Gauḍapāda and Śaṃkara, but they are just a few.

A. If I understand properly, this kind of *yoga* is little known even in India. Why is that?

R. This *yoga* belongs to the pure metaphysical order, and this implies that it is not for the many; due to its specific structure and to its operative dynamics it undoubtedly requires special qualities.

You, for example, are a painter, and we know that not everyone can paint; it is a question of aptness.

A. What kind of obstacle prevent one from following this kind of *yoga*?

R. The hardest obstacle the neophyte comes up against is that of becoming crystallized upon the plane of the empirical mind (the first level of cognitive perception). As the cognitive solution is not found by this type of *yoga* through that particular sector of the mind, one may run the risk, by going around in circles within the sphere of the analytical and critical thinking, of even becoming mad. This has happened to some philosophers who, wishing to seek truth merely on the plane of the subject-object, found themselves closed in a horizontal vicious circle of ideas and concepts up to the point of becoming frustrated and bewildered by the impossibility of finding a solution to the problem. The selective empirical mind finds its proper place and its *raison d'etre* on the plane of the horizontal line and of quantity, but if one wishes to proceed along the vertical line, sooner or later one must leave it behind and abandon it altogether. It is the first prop which begins to give way and the individual learns to live without support, bereft of his projecting mind. One must have the intelligence to understand and the courage to affirm the fact that relational thought, which one has used up to now, has completed its task and it is now time to go beyond it as something that has had its day.

A. Are there, if I may use the expression, *Asparśin* Masters?

R. Certainly, all those who, through consciential realization and not just by simple discourse, follow the pure Tradition of Śaṃkara and Gauḍapāda.

A. How can we recognize these Masters?

R. By the kind of life they reveal. A Tradition should be lived, rather than proclaimed in a sentimental and verbal manner. Only he may be said to be a *child* of *Asparśa* who lives the *Asparśa* truth. But it is easier to find *Śivaite* and *Viṣṇuite* Masters. And indeed, the majority are *Viṣṇuites*; classical *yoga* aims at achieving union with the Divinity (the *saguṇa* God-person). This means that the greater number of the *Yogins* are monists and dualists. But *Asparśa*, as we have seen, goes beyond dualism and even monism, therefore from this standpoint it is not a *yoga*; in fact in our context the word *yoga* simply means path, *sādhanā*, method, while usually it is taken in its acceptation of 'union'. The term union presupposes the idea of two entities which are to join, while in *Asparśa* there is no idea of duality at all. If we wish to give the name *yoga* to *Asparśa* we must consider it as a very special kind of *yoga*.

A. So, what is the difference between an *Asparśin*, a *bhakta* and a disciple of *Rāja-yoga*?

R. The *bhakta* moves upon the plane of sentiment, and through devotion, cult-rite and worship tries to arrive at breaking through the level of the ego and thus unites with the God-person, the giver of grace.

The *Rāja-yoga* disciple moves upon the plane of the will, and through concentration (*dhāraṇā*), meditation (*dhyāna*) and *samādhi* penetrates into the highest spheres where he unites with *puruṣa*. This is a method based on mental discipline and psychic mastering; it is a kind of *yoga* already requiring certain qualities.

The *Asparśin* moves upon the plane of the mind in its total range. He is a seeker of the ultimate Freedom, of the universal Constant, of the Pole beyond cause-effect, space and time. By discriminating between Real and non-real he arrives at the overpowering knowledge of Identity, and the realization of 'I am That'.

As you can see the first is based upon sentiment, the second upon dynamic will and the last upon knowledge at all its various levels.

As far as the final result of the *sādhanā* is concerned, we can say that the first two (together with all the other kinds of *yoga* that derive from them) attain the sphere of the *saguṇa*, while the third is directed towards *nirguṇa*.

A. Should I therefore assume that *Asparśa-yoga* is superior?

R. It is not a question of superiority or inferiority; it is a question of knowing what one wants. Everything in the universe is in its proper place and everything has its own *raison d'etre*. One may, at most, speak of degrees of Realization. The highest degree is, without doubt, the *nirguṇa* one, the one of the *constant*, of the absolute, of a-causality, of a-temporality; the exclusively metaphysical one which transcends 'nature'.

7

SAGUṆA BRAHMAN

A. What have those who have reached *saguṇa Brahman* achieved?

R. Immortality in the true sense of the word.

Saguṇa Brahman is *one* of the infinite *seeds* of *nirguṇa Brahman.* It is a seed that has naturally indefinite possibilities. Let us pay attention to the two terms: infinite and indefinite. The infinite, in its purest sense, is beyond every limit, all series, every beginning and end, every conditioning, beyond every number, every point, every line, every constraint. The indefinite, or unlimited, is a *series* of data which, although they may be extended indefinitely, are nonetheless finite and subject to the law of necessity. Thus, a series of numbers, although they can be indefinitely, combined, are nevertheless *finite.*

The Principle-seed is like the geometrical point. The point, though dimensionless, produces the line, the plane and the volume; but even though it can express itself in indefinite modes, it cannot produce other than lines, planes and volumes. The point, although belonging to the principial order, is nonetheless limitation, constraint.

Now, the *saguṇa Brahman* is a Principle-seed with indefinite expressive possibilities in both the horizontal and vertical directions. This expression is qualified and also cyclical, wherefore a *jīva* (living soul) which joins the Principle-seed follows the law of the Principle until the latter returns to *nirguṇa.*

A. What does all this mean? I do not understand.

R. Today we are living one of the *indefinite* qualified expressions of the *Īśvaric* Principle-seed. The moment will come when, due to the cyclical law that directs the Principle, this expression of universal life will enter *pralaya*, as it is called, that is into the *Īśvaric* state of sleep, into the *Īśvaric* or *Brahmanic* night, only to appear again at a new dawn.

A. If we all belong to the Principle-seed then we must all be necessarily immortal.

R. This is true. However the majority not only are unaware of this fact (because they see themselves as formal aspects) but, by becoming the slaves of their projections and of their passions, are limited to and compelled along one *particular* line of life expression. We may look at this question from another point of view: he who has realized *saguṇa* is *free* to move consciously within the indefinite vital expressions of the Principle-seed, while the non-realized one is devoid of freedom, or rather, his freedom is reduced to the bare minimum. Hence the ordinary *jīva*'s urge to look for freedom and for physical and psychological independence. But it will never be able to find freedom unless and until it transcends its own limitations which are the causes that keep it in bondage. Freedom cannot come from outside but only from within.

A. You have said 'along a particular expression of life'. Are there other expressions of life?

R. We have said that the Principle-seed contains indefinite vital expressions, one of which is precisely the human one. We know—through our sensible perception—only four expressions of life: mineral, vegetable, animal and human. But we do not know other expressions above and below them.

Man limits himself to a restricted field of existence considering it to be absolute. He deprives himself of the possibility of acceding to other modalities of life which are above the human state. He has an anthropocentric vision of life which is an act of arrogance and ignorance.

A. If the Principle-seed is one of the infinite seeds of *nirguṇa*, will it be necessary to go beyond even the Principle-seed in order to realize the unconditioned Absolute?

R. It depends upon the request of one's own heart. It depends upon the maturity of the *jīva*. It depends upon the *age* of the being.

A. Once we have reached *nirguṇa* is there no possibility to manifest oneself once again? This idea terrifies me.

R. My dear one, do not be upset. We can say that in *nirguṇa* there is Freedom, in the Principle-seed there is *necessity.* From this you can draw your own conclusions.

A. When all the indefinite modes of life that the Point-principle-seed can express are transcended, or when weariness or *old age* occurs with reference to the various orders and grades of manifest life, then a request for *returning,* in a total and integral sense, into the absolute *nirguṇa* takes place?

R. Exactly so. We can put it this way: when the individual and universal subconsciousness is transcended, the time of return has come, the prodigal Son comes back home. It is along this line that the *Asparśa* proves to be highly useful and finds its *raison d'etre.*

A. Is necessity pain?

R. Necessity is dual: in it we experiment pain and pleasure. Necessity itself is the daughter of Freedom, but only Freedom is absolute.

A. Another thought terrifies me: does not *nirguṇa Brahman* mean total annihilation?

R. The Absolute as such is neither annihilation, nor negation nor nothingness nor staticity nor any other idea the mind may possibly create. The Absolute or the Infinite, on account of its intrinsic nature, is the supreme Reality, and Reality can in no way mean non-being or nothing. On the contrary, only what is unreal cannot be, just as the empirical world is not. If you feel perplexed and anxious this is with reference to the empirical conflicting world, and not to the absolute Reality which is Bliss without objects and Reality without support.

We should remember, however, that these terms: *Brahman, Īśvara, jīva, ātman,* etc., are only names; we might use others in their place, but these too would simply be names.

Hidden behind the symbol-name there is Reality which is

Being itself, or rather, Non-being, as the Absolute can be pointed out only by means of negative attributes.

A. Yes, I understand. At the beginning I found great difficulty when reading particular texts, but now I realize that to use one or the other terminology is the same thing after all. What is important is to know what is meant by the term used.

So, the world we live in is non-real, is that not so? Is it perhaps an illusion, a nothing?

R. Not quite. We spoke before of levels of knowledge which in fact correspond to various degrees of truth. When Śaṃkara considers the empirical world to be *māyā* he wishes to point out that it is not absolute Reality but only a simple degree of truth. The term *māyā* has taken on various meanings: 'a magical act' of the great *Īśvara*, 'the appearance of things that are not', 'illusion' in the sense of transformation, of 'movement which determines appearances', and so on. In short, we can say that *māyā* is 'an apparent, form-producing movement', and it is assimilated to the 'dance' (movement) of *Śiva*; it represents the world of names and forms, it is the becoming of things. This phenomenon has its own degree of truth like, on the other hand, the one relevant to the dreaming state. Therefore it is not correct to hold that the world is an illusion, in the sense that it is a nothingness, emptiness, void. Nothingness cannot exist, precisely because it is nothing. Existence can be conceived insofar as it is relevant to something that *is*.

A. Why does *Brahman* produce this apparent movement?

R. This question concerns the nature of Being and only the irrational empirical self could bring it up. If you reflect you will realize that we can speculate upon everything except upon the nature of Being or the Constant.

The *nature* of a thing is, and we can say no more about it. The ultimate Reality excludes the possibility of questioning its nature. In the One-without-a-second there can be no questions. Remember that some questions are badly posed precisely because the mind does not understand its own nature, other questions have no reason to be and others are solved by the intervention of Knowledge.

A. However, I cannot conceive a static Reality.

R. You are still trapped by your empirical mind. Some interpret the world in terms of becoming-movement (for example, Heraclitus and a number of modern philosophers as well) and some who see it in terms of staticity, non-movement (like Parmenides and others). We have, as you can see, two philosophical conceptions that, after all, contradict one another because they rest upon concepts of relation. They are, therefore, dualistic empirical conceptions.

In the *Vedānta* vision these two concepts correspond to those of *māyā-śakti* (manifest formal movement-life) and universal principial *Īśvara* or *Puruṣa* (unmoved mover, non-manifested, informal).

Know that the Constant is the ultimate Reality where all kinds of dualism or polarity disappear. Besides it is difficult for you to conceive life as static because you are experiencing movement. In reality whoever is moving cannot conceive motionlessness and vice-versa; thus whoever lives the good cannot conceive of evil and vice-versa.

8

MĀYĀ: APPARENT MOVEMENT

A. A number of *Paṇḍitas* and Masters have called the doctrine of Śaṃkara illusionism, even in the disparaging sense of the word.

R. Let us leave aside what the opposers of Non-duality and those who do not know say. Let us look at the spirit and not at the letter of Non-dualism, and at what Śaṃkara really meant by the term *māyā*.

According to Śaṃkara and Gauḍapāda this empirical world is like a phenomenal projection produced by a fakir-magician, or the projection of a dream, or a mirage in the desert, or a rope mistaken for a snake.

Now, these factors are simply phenomena which appear and disappear. A form or a body, for example, a physical object whatsoever, and therefore a planet, a star, etc. are only body-volumes which appear and disappear. To show this to be true we do not need any philosophical or scientific demonstration, because certain things prove themselves. What value can we give to a world that is and yet is not, that appears and then disappears, exists and yet does not exist, arises and annuls itself? An absolute value? This is not possible because an absolute must be a Constant, a reality that always is, a Truth that is not subject to contradictions.

If some researchers, of any order or degree, are satisfied with dwelling upon values that are not absolute, let them do so. Gauḍapāda and Śaṃkara have undertaken the path of the universal Constant, of the universally valid, of the Real as such, and with no compromises. After all, as we have already seen, Max Planck arrived at the same conception of Reality.

Śaṃkara investigated the processes of life and found that everything in it is not constant but fragmentary and relative, and that if we wish to discover the Constant we must necessarily go beyond this phenomenal and fleeting world.

Your conflicts have become increasingly deeper because you have moved simply along the horizontal line experiencing pleasures of all kinds. The satisfaction of one pleasure kindled another, the disappointment over a pleasure spurred you into looking for another; but one conflict-pleasure added to another conflict-pleasure amounts only to two conflict-pleasures without solving the problem. It is not along the horizontal, phenomenal line that you can find peace of heart, this will come about when you shatter your 'circumference' becoming a *point* free from bondage.

A. I understand this perfectly. However, from what we have said it seems to me that Gauḍapāda's, and therefore Śaṃkara's, doctrine is a kind of philosophical phenomenism.

R. Not quite. The philosophical phenomenism holds that everything is phenomenon including Reality itself, including the individual in its wholeness.

Śaṃkara, on the contrary, argues that behind phenomena there exists that Reality which is not phenomenon, and such a Reality is the Constant without birth, time, space or cause. *Brahman* as the Absolute and the Infinite exists behind *māyā*.

A. The world we live in, then, the sufferings, the struggles, the joys, man's history, all the intellectual achievements, all is but a dream?

R. The task of every true and daring researcher is that of not interfering with the truth, which emerges from investigation, by mixing it with sentimental opinions. The consciousness should be prepared to accept things as they are, not as one wishes they were.

We know that our very same planet once had a beginning (emergence) and it will come to an end in the future (disappearance). Though the ego's consciousness refuses to believe in the disintegraton of its own 'material support' it has to surrender in the face of truth.

When we say that all we see around us, including our own material body of expression, has the consistency of a dream, this means that it appears and disappears, it means that it represents an unreal-unsubstantial framework which no sooner comes into being than it no longer is. Though the ego refuses to believe in the fleeting nature of its becoming, our deepest awareness has to recognize and accept an axiom.

A. If our struggles and our actions have no sense we arrive at a form of psychological nihilism.

R. All that is process or becoming, and therefore all that it implies, has its own value and its own degree of truth as long as we find ourselves in the process. Thus, in a dream everything has its *raison d'etre* and its own value as long as we are dreaming. Likewise, life as we have conceived it in our distinctive empirical sphere of existence has its own value as long as we are within it, but it is obvious that he who has gone beyond it cannot attribute any absolute value to it at all.

A desire and a sorrow have their value and meaning as long as they exist, but when they no longer exist neither retains any sense whatsoever and so does the object of desire or sorrow. In this case too Śaṃkara has set the question in its proper perspective: the empirical world has its meaning and its *raison d'etre* as long as we are identified with it. Therefore every human action, every ethics, every quest, etc., have their particular reason as long as we experience this life of relation or the individuality. But since this kind of life is not absolute, as it represents only a particular degree of truth, sooner or later we have to become aware of something more profound, compared to which everything else loses importance, just as a dream loses its significance when we wake up. Nobody in the waking would weep for the dead seen in the dream, as nobody would pay any attention to the arguments heard in dreaming; and as, again, nobody would dare count on a merely dreamt treasure.

A. Is the Constant or the Absolute not simply the sum of all these half-truths or grades of reality? If this is so, the empirical world, although being *māyā*, must be real.

R. The relative (non-supreme), though indefinitely summed can never give the Absolute (Supreme). A phenomenon when added to another phenomenon can never produce the Constant. A finite factor summed to another finite factor can never add up to the Infinite. A number, no matter how often multiplied, can never produce the metaphysical Zero. The relative cannot produce the Absolute, just as the phenomenon cannot give rise to the noumenon. A half-truth added to another half-truth gives us simply two half-truths.

It is true that by taking the empirical world in its entirety, with all its degrees of relative truth, we arrive at the cosmic *māyā*; and this, in fact, is what Śaṃkara says.

All the various phenomenal degrees of truth taken together amount to the *māyā* of the Lord *Īśvara*, while taken singly they are various forms of *avidyā*. Thus *avidyā* concerns the particular and *māyā* the *Īśvaric*-universal. In any case, these are just terms of reference.

A. It seems to me that Śaṃkara introduced two orders of reality: *Brahman* and *māyā*.

R. They are not exactly two orders of reality. We have said that the only real is the Absolute and the Constant, and the only Constant-Absolute is *Brahman*. A dream, for example, disappears completely leaving no traces for him who wakes up.

A. How can we connect the empirical world with *Brahman*? I mean, how can we resolve the problem of the connection between the two? If *māyā* is separated from *Brahman* we must find the cause of its origin. If it is not detached from *Brahman* then it must be a product of *Brahman*, and in this case the effect must be as real as its cause. As you see, the world must be absolute and real.

R. If we were confronted by two distinct realities naturally the problem of their connection and their relationship would arise, together with the question of establishing which one of the two should be considered as coming first. In our case, however, we are not given two distinct realities (the two distinct realities are, instead, the problem of the dualists), and therefore this problem does not concern *Advaita*.

The relationship between the two factors in question is similar to that which arises when we try to find the connection between the dream-projection and the mind-substratum in the dreaming state. A dream is only a *continuum-discontinuum* jutting out against the screen of our mind only to disappear, as mist before the wind, at the touch of waking. Thus, the empirical universe is simply a *continuum-discontinuum* which irradiates upon the screen of *Brahman*.

A. So we are not confronted by two orders of reality and therefore we must conclude, as I was saying just now, that the universe or the empirical reality (effect) is the product of *Brahman* (cause). The effect must be of the same nature of the cause, therefore the effect is real-absolute.

R. An effect, although of the same essence of the cause, is not the cause; thus a mountain conjured up by the mind in a dream or imagined while awake is not the whole mind. Let us say that the mountain is a consciential moment of the mind, but the mind is something more. The mountain comes and goes but the mental substance remains; the mountain is only *one* of the indefinite expressive potentialities or possibilities of the mind. Thus, the universal mind has projected all this empirical world which, although of the same essence as the mind, is not the universal mind in its entirety.

We said before that the *Īśvaric* Principle-seed contains countless expressions of life which represent only vital moments of the Principle-seed. Clay is more than the simple jar, just as the electronic substance is more than a particular spatial-temporal physical element. Hence the various degrees of truth which we discussed before. The formal universe is nothing but the representation of numberless picture-dreams of the great cosmic Dreamer; vibrating notes played by the great universal Musician; sketches, drawings, paintings of the great Painter; geometry of points and volumes of the principial Geometer. The error lies in considering the projected consciential moments as the Absolute as such. The mistake is to think that also the human formal consciential moment (one of the indefinite notes played by the great Musician) is absolute, whereas it is, in the totality of things, but a winking of an eye which, compared to the principial Seed, is without any value at all.

The magician, says Śaṃkara, by the power of his mind projects a rope, then an individual which climbs up the rope, followed by another individual who, holding a knife, kills the first. The onlookers on *seeing* this show are bewildered and horrified (there are some magician-fakirs who are able to give performances of this kind). Finally, like mist in the wind, the picture-image vanishes and all we can see is the fakir sitting calm and *motionless* on the ground. The empirical reality is similar to this picture-image, like this unsubstantial event, this movement which, when all is said and done, is only *apparent movement.*

Let us say a few words more about *māyā*. *Māyā* is not a substantial entity, but a fleeting, contradictory and impermanent datum; *māyā* is a verification of facts on the part of the individual; it is not even a particular theory for explaining the universe.

Māyā is apparent movement, just as the dreaming movement is apparent. Besides, we cannot look for its cause, because to look for the cause of the change in the very same change would lead us to a *reductio ad absurdum*. That apparent movement disappears instantaneously at the *realization* of being, just as, for instance, the empirical ignorance of a thing disappears instantaneously at the rise of the knowledge about the thing itself. If this is the case, that empirical ignorance could not be absolute, nor be a substantial factor nor, again, could it have a real cause because a real cause cannot produce an unreal effect.

A. So *māyā* is a limitation and therefore we must conclude that the being limits itself.

R. This is an instance of reasoning by absurd. Whether you call *māyā*: limit, superimposition, phenomenon, creative power, etc., it makes no difference: all of these are but names which, in truth, stand for a certain operative possibility.

A. I understand. However, two consequences result, namely that (1) this operative process is a form of naturalistic pantheism and, (2) *Brahman*, by transforming Itself into moments-frame-works, cannot be the constant.

R. Today I must really congratulate you, because you seem to be more like a true researcher than a prejudiced critic.

I am following your consciousness and your attitude and I believe that by stimulating one another we will be able to find out.

Pantheism, according to the philosophical view, argues that everything is nature, that there is no transcendent Entity and that all is immanent in an absolute sense.

Now, this is not the view of Non-dualism. We have already said that an image is merely a particular, spatial-temporal factor of the Principle. The Principle stands unmoved upon itself just like the magician of the example. Therefore, this condition transcends the phenomenon. In other words, the phenomenon-universe is a reflection, a projection of the Seed-principle which remains transcendent and non-manifested. Thus, we have that which is manifested and objective and that which is no-manifested and subjective, what appears and what remains hidden, what is phenomenon and what is noumenon. Rather than of pantheism we might speak of 'panentheism'.

Besides, we should bear in mind that this principle is only one of the infinite reflections of *nirguṇa Brahman*, which totally transcends both the Seed-principle and the projective development proceeding from it.

Therefore, we have the formal life, the Seed-principle (phenomenon and noumenon) and, finally, the root of both, the absolute Constant. We should not take what is form and life for the root of both or, in other words (just to give names to these things), *nirguṇa Brahman, saguṇa Brahman* and the world of names and forms.

A. Since Non-duality, *Asparśa* or *Advaita*, supports the

non-generation and the a-causality of everything, how can we reconcile this affirmation with what we have just said?

R. Apparently there seems to be a contradiction, but in fact it is not so. By the term 'birth' we mean a 'coming forth', a 'springing from something in order to start being'. Thus we say that an individual is born in the sense that he has come into existence and has an autonomous life of his own.

If one looks at things properly, the universe did not 'come forth' from *saguṇa Brahman* so as to have an absolute life of its own. The universe or cosmic dream is only an 'ideal modification' of the *Īśvaric* mind, just as a dream is a thought movement of the dreamer's mind. The image-pictures of the dreamer do not come out from his reality to become another autonomous and absolute reality. The dreamed mountain is nothing but an objective idea of the sleeping mind; ice is but a modification of water and it has never abandoned the water element to take on an independent and absolute existence of its own. The Principle cannot abandon its own principial nature.

The question being thus formulated, we cannot speak of birth, of generation of something, because in actual fact nothing is born, as all is simply the ideal modification of the universal Mind.

A. In this case we affirm an absolute idealism or mentalism.

R. This is not true either, because the universal Mind or, as it is called in *Vedāntic* terms, *prakṛti* or *pradhāna*, is a pole of the *Īśvaric* dyad, which is formed by *puruṣa* (positive pole) and *prakṛti* (negative pole). *Prakṛti* symbolizes the cosmic 'Mother', that Mother through which phenomena emerge, while *puruṣa* represents the stimulator. In other words, they are the father-mother of every Tradition.

For greater clarity we can sum everything up in the following scheme:

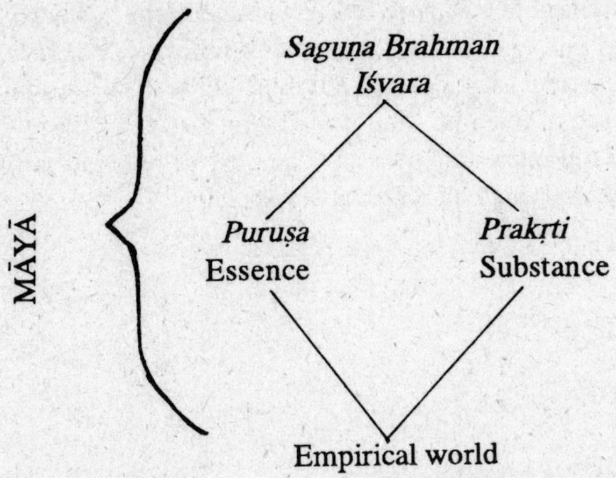

A. If everything is *māyā*, even the individual is *māyā*; therefore the sentence 'Tat Tvam Asi' is senseless.

R. When the dreaming mind projects a *jīva*-subject and this identifies with the objective dream world and with its own qualifications, we could say to it: "Beware, you are neither that nor these, your identifications are the outcome of ignorance-*avidyā*; in reality *you are the mind.*" Thus, to the individual who identifies himself with his projections: body, sense-organs and various objects, we say: "Beware, you are not these transient things; you are, instead, the Constant, the root of your own essence". This world of *māyā* superimposes itself upon the pure Essence-Constant and *Asparśa* Realization consists precisely in finding again our true nature of Being. This is the most precious gift that can be offered to the individual in conflict. The *Asparśa* message aims at making us remember that we are of the same nature as the absolute Constant. We are Existence, Consciousness and Bliss absolute, but the identification with what we are not leads us into conflict and suffering. Man believes he is the body, desire, intellect, etc., but these things are only different aspects of illusion-*māyā*; behind these distorting appearances there is the true Being, that which was never born and which will never cease to be.

We have seen that the *Saguṇa*-seed is a reflection, a 'chiaroscuro' standing out against the screen of the infinite *Brahman*, which is the one and only Reality, the One-without-a-second, the true absolute Constant. The *jīva* (living soul) is simply a chiaroscuro of the universal *jīva*, and this, as we have already said, is but a chiaroscuro of *nirguṇa Brahman*.

9

EVOLUTIONISM

A. I have reflected and meditated a lot about the things we spoke of last. I was asking myself lately whether the vision that you have expounded to me comes from Śaṃkara.

R. Śaṃkara has only evidenced what the *Śruti* (the *Vedas* and the *Upaniṣads*) says. In fact, the concepts of *māyā,* of the One-without-a-second, etc., are all to be found in the *Śruti.*

For example, it is stated that:

"Because wherever there is, as it were, duality, wherever there is a second, there one beholds the other, there one knows the other; but wherever all this (dualism) has resolved into the *ātman,* how can one see the other and how can one know the other?"

(*Bṛhadāraṇyaka Upaniṣad*: II, iv, 14)

"Indra, by means of *māyā,* appears to be universe."

(*Ṛg. Veda*: VI, xlvii, 18)

"... All the various modifications being merely distinctions of names and speech..."

(*Chāndogya Upaniṣad*: VI, i, 4)

"In truth, o Satyakāma, OM is the supreme *Brahman* as well as the non-supreme *Brahman.*"

(*Praśna Upaniṣad*: V, 2)

"Not this, not this" (speaking about the impossibility of describing the supreme *Brahman*).

(*Bṛhadāraṇyaka Upaniṣad*: IV, vi, 22—IV, v, 15)

"... the one, before which the words recede..."

(*Taittirīya Upaniṣad*: II, 9)

"That which is different both from the known and the unknown."

(*Kena Upaniṣad*: I, 4)

"It is the supreme *Brahman*, beginningless, known as neither existing nor non-existing."

(*Bhagavadgītā*: XIII, 12)

"That thou art."

(*Chāndogya Upaniṣad* : VI, ix, 4)

"It is at once within and without, it is causeless."

(*Muṇḍaka Upaniṣad*: II, ii, 2)

"It is all that is."

(*Chāndogya Upaniṣad*: VII, xxv, 2)

"You know it as Being and as non-being."

(*Muṇḍaka Upaniṣad*: II, iii, 1)

A. Does this world of *māyā* evolve, has it a purpose of its own? For sometime now I have been posing myself the question of life's evolution and, in truth, I am perplexed by it.

R. The Absolute does not need to evolve, a Constant which evolves is no Constant, an Infinite with a *purpose* is not a complete Infinite. Therefore, that which could possibly evolve is *māyā*, but *māyā*-phenomenon has no specific aim of its own, no purposefulness because it disappears as if by magic at the touch of *Brahmanic* Realization.

Thus, the nocturnal dream has no real purpose, it vanishes on awaking. We can say that the *māyā*-universe, as a *continuum-discontinuum*, can be interrupted at any given moment.

He who sets himself a goal and a purpose is the unfulfilled one who is not, who is lacking something, who is incomplete. But the Absolute, being completeness and fullness, needs neither development nor the acquisition of something through a possible finalized purpose.

A. So life, being devoid of any and all purposes, is meaningless.

R. Life is nonsense when compared to the Absolute or the Constant, but not when the *jīva* is *within* life. We have said that a desire has its motive as long as it lasts; but when it disappears the problem of whether it had any import or not becomes meaningless. The same holds true for this particular expression of life; when *Brahman* is realized the problem of measuring its validity need no longer be posed. When the effect disappears, the cause disappears too, and the without-cause is, obviously, beyond any cause.

The individual, being cause-time-space, conceives all in terms of evolution and purpose. It is difficult for him to think of a Reality which is neither time nor space nor history nor aim. Actually, he cannot think of it because this kind of Reality cannot be imagined, it can only be realized.

An ego-*māyā*, precisely because it is not, sets itself certain goals and aims; it tries to develop, to expand; but no matter what goals and aims it is shooting for, it will always be an ego-*māyā*. A relative, though it may try to surpass itself, remains always relative. In fact, the ego-*māyā* lives and perpetuates itself in the pursuit of its ideals and as it is not capable of living without these compensations it believes that the Absolute too must depend upon contingent compensatory factors. In other words, it makes its problems absolute, it anthropomorphizes the unqualified, a-causal Constant.

Therefore, terms such as time-space, evolution-history, aim-purpose, cause-effect, etc., are all words concerning relative data which belong to the world of *māyā*; they vanish at the touch of *Brahmanic* Realization.

10

UNITY OF TRADITION

A. I would have preferred to live in silence today, but I am here to make you a gift of a number of thoughts that I have been carrying within me for some time now, that is since I met a friend who spoke to me about Western traditional Teaching. You see, I would like to understand if the vision of the One-without-a-second belongs exclusively to the *Advaita* tradition, or if it is presented also by other traditions.

R. In other words your question is: does Truth belong to *Advaita* only?

A. Yes, I think that that is what I mean.

R. You have put your finger upon a very fine point. All the followers of a specific credo, of a particular kind of *yoga*, of a religion, etc., think they are the sole depositary of the Truth and, as a result, they feel they have the exclusive right to 'exploit' it. There are many who are scholars or experts, at a cultural level, of particular doctrines, and often they too become sectarian. Thus we have people who are 'fanatical' about the music of Beethoven, Brahms, Verdi, etc.

There are people who are 'fanatical' about the Vedic culture, the *Upaniṣads*, the *Purāṇa* or about the Jewish, Egyptian, Rosicrucian, Christian, Moslem, etc., culture. There are the 'fanatics' about certain rather special languages such as Sanskrit and Hebrew which, it is said, are the languages of the Gods. We must, first of all, make a distinction: there are teachings at the individual or personalistic level, and teachings at traditional level, which is of a universal and principial order.

The traditional unity is guaranteed by its fundamental note which is supraindividual and suprarational-sensible (above the rational mind and the senses). Tradition should not be mistaken for the historical, social and cultural traditionalism of a people. The Tradition we speak about has nothing to do with the traditional conservatorism of a nation or of a religion. It is important to understand what it is meant by Tradition because much confusion has arisen and is bound to arise about this term, both in good and bad faith.

Plato, Gauḍapāda, Śaṃkara, etc., have all taught the traditional Knowledge. Tradition, although one, has many branches. It may be compared to a tree: the trunk is the one life of Tradition while the branches represent its various spatial-temporal adaptations or presentations.

As long as the consciousness of the neophyte, who is following a particular branch, does not understand the true vital core of Tradition, he will consider that specific branch as the one and only trustworthy branch, and at times he may even oppose the other branches considering them as non-traditional. Hence that brand of fanaticism which emerges from the misunderstanding of the one traditional Doctrine.

We must also point out that some branches, due to the incompleteness of their seekers, may have known degenerations of various kinds.

A. Who is it, then, that creates these distinctions?

R. It is the sense of ego (*ahaṃkāra*). When the sense of ego disappears all can be seen in perfect Unity.

The one consciousness sees the apparent multiplicity as unity; I say 'apparent' because every possible distinction is not absolute but it is considered absolute because it is observed from a particular point of view.

A. It may be that not all these branches of Tradition tend towards the ultimate Truth; I mean, along the way they may lose sight of the supreme goal.

R. Every true branch of Tradition represents a complete teaching, even though the various followers of a given teaching may dwell on some particular or lesser aspects of it. What degenerates the Doctrine (*Śruti*), as we have pointed out before, is devotional and fanatical sentimentalism, and sterile, dogmatic, critical, separative and arrogant intellectualism. At times these two aspects may even be found hand in hand.

The *Sermon on the Mount* and the *Māṇḍūkya Upaniṣad* are not to be approached with emotional or intellectual-*manasic* premises.

Let us take the Cabbalistic Teaching. As you probably know, *Qabbālāh* means 'oral tradition' and its key symbol is the Sephirothic Tree. By studying, meditating and contemplating this symbol we can become illuminated with regard to many things, at various cognitive levels. In it we have three Aspects-principles which are equivalent to the three principles of the Hindu Doctrine: *Śiva-Viṣṇu-Brahmā.* They are Kether (*Śiva*), Chokmah (*Viṣṇu*) and Binah (*Brahmā*).

Kether is the principial One and it also corresponds to the *Vedānta*'s *saguṇa Brahman.*

A. But *nirguṇa Brahman*, that is the strictly metaphysical aspect which is the one that most interests us, is missing.

R. It is not missing. It exists under the name of *Ain-soph-aur*, which can be understood in terms of 'negatives'. In other words it stands for Non-being, while Kether is the primordial determination; on the Tree of Life it stands at the very top, above Kether.

All the *Sephiroth* are simply 'modifications' of Kether, 'ideas' of Kether, and the idea is associated with the number. For *Vedānta* too, the universe is merely the 'modification' of *Īśvara* or *saguṇa Brahman.*

A. Are there Cabbalists who follow the pathway of *Ain-soph*?

R. The West is more objectivistic, I might add, more materialistic; it is more occultist than metaphysical. Many Cabbalists propose the pathway of Yesod, of Netzah, of Hod which are aspects of inter-individualism and do not even rise to the level of Tephereth; therefore, we are a long way from the metaphysical Path. Even though in the Cabbalistic *Maṇḍala*-tree there is a pathway or 'Way of the Arrow', which is the Path of Fire, only the very few follow it.

A. Is there a 'Path of Fire' in the *Qabbālāh* too?

R. The midway Path of the Tree is in reality the 'Path of Fire'.

The 'Path of Fire', which you know by now, is not a new teaching (how could it be if we have said that traditional Knowledge is not the fruit of human thinking?), it is not personal or individual, it is not doctrinaire syncretism, but represents the 'Universal Way' of realization, the essence, because after all every traditional branch proves to be a Path of Fire.

There is not practical teaching that is not connected with fire.

The East speaks of *Śakti*-fire, the West of 'Fires that consume', of alchemic Fire, of solar Fire (Rā), of '*philosophia per ignem*' and science speaks of electronic fire, etc.

Let us read these verses from the *Kaṭha Upaniṣad* (I, 13-14-15).

«"O Yama, you know the Fire that leads to Heaven, disclose It to me as I am full of Faith."

"I will teach you that Fire, o Naciketas, that can raise you to Heaven. Know that Fire is the means to win infinite worlds; It is their very foundation and It is hidden in a secret place."

He then taught him that Fire, source of the world».

The Path of Fire is the way that all disciples follow, whatever traditional branch they may belong to; but its denomination remains nonetheless within the ambit of names and language.

A. Then the ultimate Truth does not belong exclusively to *Vedānta*.

R. Truth is everyone's and it belongs to everybody. Truth is Freedom and Freedom cannot be exclusive, have limitations or be sectarian.

There can be, however, some Great Souls who have revealed metaphysical Truth in its essence. Two of these Souls are, in fact, Gauḍapāda and Śaṃkara. This is why I have spoken to you of *Advaita* and of *Asparśa-yoga*.

A. Can you tell me of anybody in the West who spoke, let us say, in *Advaita* terms?

R. If we wish to give a beginning to these things we can refer to Parmenides, the Eleatic philosopher (540 B.C.).

Here is what Prof. P. Lamanna writes in his *Storia della Filosofia* (Le Monnier, Firenze):

"... Milesians and Pythagoreans had asked themselves: what is the principle of the universe? That is, what is the substance or the unifying force of the universe, that which makes the world not mere disjointed agglomeration of fragments but a whole? And Xenophanes now replies: the One.

What is, they asked themselves, the deeper nature of Being? And Parmenides now replies: the Being. The Ionians and the Pythagoreans has singled out water, fire, air, number: they were therefore in disagreement with one another about the determination of the specific nature and the essential properties of reality. But this remains certain, that water or air or fire or number is Being, and that Being is.

Therefore, all those determinations of reality which would imply non-being are to be excluded as mere appearance. It follows that the multiplicity of things is unreal and illusory, because this implies that one thing, by being distinct from the others, is not the others; every transformation or movement, and in general every becoming, is unreal and illusory, implying that an object that becomes is (in a moment) what it is not (a moment later). But sensible experience in fact presents reality to us as a complex of objects each one distinct from the other, each one including a multiplicity of parts and qualities for ever changing, having a beginning and an end, that is, subject to birth and death. Therefore, sensible experience is but a web of illusions; it must be abandoned in order to follow 'reason'".

Let us now read some rather significant fragments. Plutarch writes about Parmenides: "He declares in fact that according to the truth of things, the whole is eternal and unchanging; in fact it is totally whole, one, still and ungenerated. Becoming, on the other hand, concerns things that seem to exist from a false point of view. Sensations he excludes from the ambit of truth. He says that if there is something beyond being, this is not being; but non-being does not exist absolutely. In this way he arrives to pose the ungenerated being."

And Aristotle when speaking of the Eleatic philosophers says:

"Some of them negated generation and corruption altogether; in fact they said that nothing among the entities is either generated or perishes, but it only seems so to us".

Timon says of Parmenides: "The solitary power of Parmenides, the lion-hearted, who diverted the mind from the fraud of representations".

And again concerning Parmenides: "... vice-versa being must be grasped through thought, the Logos, the only instrument that permits us to grasp, through the very immutability of the word itself, the being as a complete, perfect and changeless identity, surpassing the illusory nature of changeable and contradictory opinion...." (A distinction is made between superconscious, intellectual knowledge and simple opinion which arises from imperfect senses). "For his affirmation of the absolute superiority of the way of thought compared to that of opinion, and for believing in the ontological import of the Logos, Parmenides is of vital importance in the history of Greek philosophy, in that he was one of the first to identify word and essence and to find in logical judgment the instrument by which to understand the rationality of the real. In this perspective he is also assigned the discovery of the formal principles such as those of identity and non-contradiction, which will form the basis of all the successive rationalistic or idealistic elaborations." (From *Dizionario di Filosofia*, Rizzoli 1976)

And Diogenes Laertes writes of Melissos, one of Parmenides' disciples: "He thinks that all is infinite and unchanging and motionless and one, homogeneous in itself and full; that motion does not exist but is only appearance."

And Melissos says: "... instead it seems to us that heat becomes cold and cold heat, that hardness becomes softness and softness hardness, that the living dies and comes from the non-living, and that all things change and that what was and what now is are not at all equal; in fact, iron, that is indeed hard, is consumed by the contact with our fingers, and the same is for gold and stones and every other thing which seems resistant, and that, on the contrary, earth and stones come from water. And as a result it is inevitable that we neither see nor know reality. Because there is certainly no agreement on all this. While we say that things are many and eternal and have certain aspects of resistance, it seems to us that all is changing and different every time we look at it again. It is clear therefore that we did not see rightly and that those things did not rightly seem to be multiple; in fact they would not change if they were real, but each would remain exactly what it was. Nothing is stronger than what really exists. But if it changes, behold the being dies and non-being is born.

So, therefore, if there were multiplicity, it would have to be exactly like the one". (These fragments are taken from *I Presocratici*, vol. I, Laterza, Bari)

A. I am astonished. I seem to recognize in this the *Advaita* or the *Asparśa-yoga* view. If you had not mentioned the names of Parmenides, Melissos, etc., I would certainly have thought of Śaṃkara and Gauḍapāda.

R. Doubtless these two metaphysical views have many points in common, although they are not identical. We do not need to go into the differences, also due to the fact that of the Eleatic school we have only a few fragments. On the other hand, at that time many things were transmitted orally and other things distorted on purpose so as not to clash with current opinion or because they would have not been properly understood. We do not even know whether the teachings of Pythagoras, Socrates, Plato etc. are all we have in our hands now or whether there is more, perhaps of even greater importance.

And this is what Plotinus (204-270 A.D.), the most eminent Neoplatonic thinker of the Roman-Alexandrine school, says:

"We should be spectators of murders, and all deaths, and takings and sackings of cities, as if they were on the stages of theatres, all changes of scenery and costume and acted wailings and weepings. For really here in the events of our life it is not the soul within but the outside shadow of man which cries and moans and carries on in every sort of way on a stage which is the whole of earth where men have in many places set up their stages. Doings like these belong to a man who knows how to live only the lower and external life and is not aware that he, after all, is just playing—even his tears, also when he sheds serious tears, are but a play. For only the seriously good part of man is capable of taking serious doings seriously; the rest of man is a toy. But toys too, are taken seriously by those who do not know how to be serious and are toys themselves. But if anyone joins in their play and suffers their sort of sufferings he must know that he has tumbled into a children's game and put off the playcostume in which he was dressed." (*Enneads*: III, 2, xv)

As you can see there are some analogies with the *Bhagavad-gītā* and with the Hindu vision of the *līlā* (divine game).

Plotinus' One (*That* or *turīya* of the *Vedānta*) is beyond action, beyond the body, beyond the Soul, beyond the Spirit itself: "Because, only after Him came Spirit and fullness, which needed both to satisfy themselves and to think".

And more: "... In conclusion we must exclude thinking from the One: such an addition would in fact be a subtraction and a deficiency... But if you grasp it by taking away being from it, you will be filled with wonder."

"There is a difference between one thing thinking another and something thinking itself; the latter goes further towards escaping being two... It becomes a pair, therefore, while remaining one." (*Enneads* III, 8, x and V, 6, i)

"But here what underlies is sterile and inadequate to be being, because the others do not come from it, but it is a shadow, and upon what is itself a shadow, a picture and a seeming." (*Enneads* VI, 3, viii)

I think we need to make no comment.

Let us now read something regarding Spinoza, the philosopher born at Amsterdam in 1632; we are already in an era when the concept of philosophy is no longer that of Tradition.

"But has this whole process, in which the eternal becomes temporal and the infinite determines itself in transient modes, any objective reality, or is it a world of appearances caused by the imperfection of the standpoint from which we look at reality?"

"Without doubt, the distinction between our two ways of considering the divine reality is essential to the Spinozian system. The one is that belonging to the imagination which isolates the single modes from the divine unity and totality and links them one another in an endless chain of successive phenomena, which cannot but remain fragmentary and for ever incomplete. The other is that of the intellect which, making rid of the limitations of time, quantity and number, reabsorbs all the manifestations of being into the eternal and indivisible unity of the divine substance: it sees the reality of each thing not in what in it is changing and fleeting in any given moment, but in its changeless essence, *sub specie aeternitatis*.... And if some things appear to us to be simply possible or contingent, this, indeed, is the effect—the only effect—of our ignorance or rather of the superimposing upon the intellect of our imagination, which leads us into mistaking the relative for the absolute, and what is partial and fragmentary for the totality." (P. Lamanna: *Storia della Filosofia*, vol. II - F. Le Monnier, Firenze)

As you can see they speak of ignorance (*avidyā*), of superimposition (*adhyāsa*), of imagination (*vikṣepa-śakti*); in the sense in which they are used, these terms are analogous to those used by *Vedānta*. Well, let us stop our readings here, and you, on your own, can take them up again later on.

A. I am happy to have listened to some concepts of these philosophers. Besides, I am convinced that man, the thinking, rational man, has always tried to understand himself and life.

Now more than ever I feel that all serious research must be directed at the discovery of the true nature of Being. All postponements or deviations mean evading the basic problem, which in turn cannot but lead one into conflict and suffering. I realize that the philosophical views proposed by many human personalities have many points of contact and affinity, even of identity. This helps me also to understand that the knowledge is one and one is the object of knowledge.

R. Many have said the same things, though in different ways, using arguments of their own, with a conceptual methodology suitable to the time and to the particular type of education received by the author, and with different nuances. This does not imply—let us say it again—that there are no differences.

It is our task—we who aim at Realization—to go to the *essence* of all Doctrines because we know that as Truth is one, so is Tradition one, even though they both may be seen from numerous, apparently different points of view. We must leave behind all discussions concerning the phenomenal process of becoming and place ourselves upon the plane of Being; in other words we must place the Philosophy of Being at the very basis of our enquiry and of our realization.

11

BODILY DEATH

A. I am here again after a very sad interval. The death of one of my brothers has shaken me considerably. I must admit that it has been a trying experience. When we lose certain things and certain persons we lose something of ourselves. It seems impossible that my brother is no longer here, impossible not to see him, speak to him.... It seems impossible to me that one moment a person exists, walks about, speaks and then is gone. At home at times I seem to see him, I am almost on the point of speaking to him and then I realize that he is no longer here. What a terrible anguish! Death does create suffering, an unspeakable torment. Why must we die?

R. Because we are born.

A. No, I beg of you, do not speak of philosophy today. Try to understand the state I am in. Help me, give me a hand with forgetting the anguishing plight that oppresses and suffocates me.

R. Love does not allow me to leave you in this state; but do you really think that I can solve your trouble by simply patting you on the shoulder and consoling you in a sentimental way?

A. I have not got the strength to think, to discriminate, to sythesize. Can you not see that I am at a loss?

R. You have been a revolutionary and you fear death! What a strange association. Let us meditate a while, we shall take up our discussion later on.

* * *

A. My sadness derives from two events which I place, the one in the physical, the other in the psychical-emotional sphere. I am saddened by the disappearance of the form in itself which fact in turn has caused me suffering at the psychological level because it deprived me a source of affection, of a relationship.

R. Thus, we have anguish due to the disappearance of a form and that which derives from the loss of affection. Wherever there is attachment to any body-form there is also suffering. Attachment bears in itself the seed of suffering. Attachment consists in assimilation with the object and assimilation coincides with *possession.*

This process often works as an unconscious motive, as in the case of the attachment to our own body or to other people's bodies. Attachment to a form, whether one's own or that of others, implies desiring that form, and losing it means frustrating the desire for possession.

Unconsciously the ego acts as if its possession-desire should last for ever. It would like its posses- sions to last in time, or as long as the form-desire-attachment subsists. We can be attached to the world of forms, or to that of sentiments, or to the heavenly world and so on.

These are all attachments and where there is attachment there is desire, where there is desire there is possession and where there is possession there is *māyā*, because we know very well that in the various worlds there is nothing that does not undergo movement, change or transformation. All objects of desire are transient, passing, fleeting, and to become attached to an object which is and then is no more, to become attached to a non-permanent thing and at the same time demand a permanent relationship of it is a logical absurdity. In this world of fleetingness we can possess something—a form, a relationship, etc.—only to lose it.

But the most important discovery is that which makes us recognize both the object and the subject of desire as impermanent.

My dear one, the way of possession is the way of pure illusion, of conflict and of pain, it is the way of *māyā*. Human conviction founded upon attachment is non-real, because it rests on *avidyā*.

Swāmi Vivekānanda in his *Jñāna-yoga* says: "Then there is the grandiose fact of death. The whole world walks towards death. Everything dies. Our progress, our vacuities, our reforms, our luxuries, our wealth, our erudition, all have a feature in common: death. It is the only certainty. Cities rise and disappear, empires grow and crumble; planets fall to pieces and turn into dust to vanish in the sky. And this is the way things have always been. Death is at the end of all things: of life, of beauty, of wealth, of power, even of virtue. Saints and sinners die, beggars and kings alike. All travel towards death. Yet there is in us an irresistible attachment to life, we do not know how to renounce it: and this is *māyā*."

A. I acknowledge the truth of all you say, but at the present moment I am too overcome by the identification with my sorrow, by the loss of what meant my brother.

R. This is the fundamental mistake: why do you say *my*? *My* is related to your, his, hers, etc. *My* implies possession, attachment, greed. As long as an object-form finds a response in a *my*, that object is a source of pain and conflict, often shattering pain and conflict. Nothing belongs to an ego; the concept of belonging is an illusion.

A body-object is merely movement and belongs to movement; this means that *māyā* belongs to *māyā*. What we call your or my body is simply a chiaroscuro which no sooner appears than it disappears. How can we make the impermanent eternal? To want to possess or stop movement is like trying to clutch the air.

A. I do understand. Why am I compelled by identification and possession?

R. This is a completely different question. In order to live, the ego needs to adhere to something. Due to its intrinsic nature the ego cannot live autonomously; being a relative it is subject to relativity and dependence. As long as you express yourself as ego you cannot but identify with something, you have to depend on something positive or negative, be it a subconscious content or an external factor. The ego is a *single* entity which expresses itself in terms of exclusiveness; on the plane of relationship it considers the *other* as an object of enjoyment and satisfaction.

A. Therefore, I must conclude that my closeness to my brother was and is merely the closeness between two egos, is that not so? As long as my attitude towards life is expressed in terms of 'I-you', should I assume that I shall necessarily come up against conflict and pain?

R. There is no doubt about it. There are certain laws, within the region of the universal and the particular, which, if disattended, lead inevitably into conflict.

A. In my case which is the law?

R. Where there is an ego which desires, compares, excludes, which loves possession, vanity, identification with the objects, etc., where there is an ego which, in order to feed on its gratifications, wants to keep alive who has chosen death, there you will find a breach of the law and therefore conflict and pain.

A. Now you have placed me on the opposite side. I am suffering because I am an egoist. I would have liked, in other words, to hold back my brother in order to gratify my need for love, is that not so?

R. Do not ask me but your consciousness, in the secret of your heart.

A. If life is governed by laws, then their non-knowledge is the cause favouring the breach of the laws themselves. From this point of view, what meaning can be given to 'sin' as we understand it?

R. Science, both sacred and lay, tells us that the universe is governed by laws which concern the physical (*Virāṭ*), the psychic (*Hiraṇyagarbha*) and the spiritual (*Īśvara*) spheres; every time the individual breaks one of these laws he receives back a counterblow proportionate in strength to the cause he has set in motion.

Thus, if we put our finger in the fire we receive a counterblow in the form of a burn, because both the finger and the fire are governed by precise laws. At the psychic level an ego which considers the others and the world around it as simple objects to be possessed exclusively and for its own pleasure, sooner or later will receive a reaction characterized by suffering and anguish.

My dear one, I would like to point out that I am not talking about morality, ethics and such like, as proposed by society; I am talking about the laws, norms of a universal order which are not the fruit of human invention.

What is it that causes a law, a norm to be broken? Without doubt it is ignorance, and you are already of this opinion. Whoever ignores does not know and whoever does not know can only expect conflict and pain.

Ignorance is not an excuse for acquiring merit. The law does not admit of ignorance. Your non-knowledge of certain psychic laws has landed you in suffering. Today you are crying in pain because you failed to understand the law which governs two individualities and the world of the ego. But ignorance is not absolute and it is up to you to remove it.

A. Therefore, if I have understood the law I should no longer suffer. But I realize that even though I have understood I am still suffering.

R. A law is truly understood only when it is *applied*; it is not enough to simply be acquainted with it. The law has to be put into practice, otherwise it is as if it were not known. What is the use of knowing that desire leads to suffering if you go on desiring? I am convinced that if you obey the law we have spoken of today your suffering will disappear, as you have removed the cause of the breach, that is, ignorance.

12

HARMONY

A. From what we have said so far we can conclude that *Advaita*, or *Asparśa*, is neither theology nor religion nor philosophical realism nor idealism nor pantheism. Is that not so?

R. Let us say that, in reality, it agrees with the theological, religious, idealistic and realistic aspects, but not in an absolute way. This means that these aspects may have their validity under certain circumstances; they are simple sets of co-ordinates. We can say that *Advaita* expresses itself through the law of Harmony.

A. I do not understand. What is this Harmony?

R. Harmony is based upon the synthesis of knowledge, upon the understanding that all dualisms, in the long run, are but polarities that dissolve into Unity. This vision rests also on the idea of Beauty meant as Accord among all the manifested notes. Thus, ego and non-ego, good and evil, *saṃsāra* and *nirvāṇa*, individual and universal, fact and finality, cause and effect, being and image, etc., are all *comprehended* by and resolved into the principial Unity. Harmony disregards the existence of ugliness, of separateness and conflict in the ordinary sense. Harmony conceived thus is total understanding and therefore non-opposition.

A pure *Asparśin* is Harmony in action, expressing Beauty and Accord. From this stems his non-opposition to life, even *māyika* life; from here comes his freedom which, obviously, is not the freedom *of* the ego. A pure *Asparśin* is a fulfilled one, and fulfilment does not depend on any action. As you can see, Harmony, Beauty, Esthetic sense, etc, for the *Asparśin* are not mere mental categories but expressions of life. For Tradition, Esthetics is a 'way of life'. A *sādhanā* is simply a practice aimed at revealing Accord, an instrument to express Harmony. The individual and the universe are made of vibrating notes and the disciple must have the capacity of 'hearing' the just consonance between the micro- and the macro-cosmos.

A. What are, after all, *Advaita Vedānta* and *Asparśa-yoga*?

R. They are *Advaita Vedānta* and *Asparśa-yoga*, they are pure metaphysics, non-human Tradition, Knowledge of identity; they represent a pathway which leads to the Realization of the integral Being, they are the 'Way of Fire' which reveals the Bliss and the Freedom of That, eternally non-born; they reveal identity with the Constant upon which all things depend and to which all things return.

* * *

A. I have meditated a lot upon what we said, and during these past months many things have become clear to me; various doubts have vanished, and not having sought drugs any longer I feel more tranquil and free from conflict. I believe in the existence of a Reality-Constant; I am convinced that life, as I have conceived of it up to now, is absurd; I am certain that man has only one way by which to solve his basic problems: the transformation of his own consciousness, the conquest of his innner being, his essential re-unification. His conflict cannot cease until he finds himself within himself. There is no sensible pleasure, there is no drug, no company of friends, no financial, political and worldly goods acquisition, etc., that can possibly give back to him his true dimension, his true status as a being, his integrality, his unity. Every sensory passion, however noble, is mere compensation. Sensory love at every level and degree is only love of oneself as ego-illusion.

Since I am convinced of my noumenal completeness, I would like to go on to the practical application of what we have said; in other words I wish to establish my consciousness upon the essence of my total being. I would like to take up this second cycle of conversations by speaking about other aspects of the *Asparśa* discipline which I find truly suited to my mind and my consciousness.

I venture to say that I am beginning to experience joy of heart and I think that this is true joy because it does not depend on anything, it is not the outcome of profane acquisitions or the effect of drugs, but is the result of *understanding* which calms and pacifies, which tranquillizes and places one in a state of placidity and passionlessness. I realize that self-knowledge is the basis for one's own discovery, just as I realize that understanding must touch the most profound element of oneself and not stop merely at the level of the ego-illusion's problems. And today I can say that it is no longer my despair that urges me to accept you, but my awareness. Thus, it is with joy and openness that I take up once more this dialogue with you.

Could you tell me what qualifications are required to follow thoroughly the *Asparśa-yoga*? First, however, I would like to tell you about a dream or better, dream experiences which I am having recently with a certain frequency. In most cases I find myself wandering with other people in underground places. Some time ago I was wandering about in a labyrinth and I could not find the exit. Another time I was in an underground shopping centre where I stepped on a lift which was going to the lower floors. At the peak of the experience I wake up nearly always suddenly, because there are barriers in my way that I cannot overcome. They are very vivid experiences and emotionally very strong. Never before I had such luminous, vivid and animated dreams.

Not long after we began our dialogue I had a dream in which I was having a fist-fight with another individual. I was quarrelling and fighting desperately with a person, whom I did not know at all, in an abandoned house until we were both out for the count.

13

THE QUALIFICATIONS OF THE DISCIPLE

R. Let us start with the qualifications of the disciple. The first is an intense thirst for Liberation. It must be so powerful as to condition the entire complex of the individual's psychic energies. When the fire of aspiration reaches the proper level of development, every obstacle is burnt without difficulty. Realization yields to those who truly love it. *Asparśa-yoga* is not for the weak, for the tepid or for those who wish to acquire psychic powers or missionary fervour. If there is a burning thirst for a total solution of the existential problems at all levels and degrees, then one is ready to travel up the road of no return.

The second quality is that of knowing how to withdraw inwardly, thus creating an adequate meditating attitude susceptible of further possibilities.

The third quality consists in finding in oneself the *courage* to remain deaf towards all that the world and society offer with regard to customs, social morality, literature, politics and all other expressions concerning human social condition. Later on one may return to this dimension, but with a radically changed consciousness.

The fourth regards the 'feeling' for *research* characterized by the mental discrimination between real and non-real. This implies a feeling for knowledge.

The fifth quality is that of adhering to the Truth perceived.

For *Asparśa-yoga*, Realization and ultimate Truth or Reality are one and the same thing. Liberation is achieved when one's consciousness reveals itself as Reality; in this perspective knowledge becomes consciousness. Love for Liberation is thus love for pure Reality.

Besides, it would be advisable not to set oneself limits of time, or to imagine that Realization should materialize according to one's preconceived sentimental ideas, or to give much importance to one's social-educational upbringing.

Your dream experiences are very interesting indeed. Something is moving. The *other* which you were fighting with was simply another part of yourself.

A. On the one hand I feel a strong need for a retreat, for solitude, for withdrawing into myself; yet, on the other, I realize that the force of habit urges me to go outside of myself, to go in search of contacts and relationships.

How can I solve this conflicting tendency?

R. Every time an individual is engaged in something creative he cannot help going back within himself, and this is because the real treasures are within, not without, our heart. Every enquirer, whether on a scientific, philosophical, religious, etc. level, seeks solitude as the source of intuition and meditation.

Therefore you should not be surprised if your consciousness wishes to sink in itself and find the right mode of approach to the transcendent. The fact that you feel the impulse to go outside of yourself means that in the past you have steadily pushed your psychic movement along a line of behaviour that today is conditioning you. You speak of habits and I agree with you; in *yoga* they speak of *tamasic* forces which are, in other terms, inertial forces. What matters now is not to divert your attention away from your 're-entry' move. What you need now is *vigilance.* In the word vigilance you will find the key to your problem, and not just your immediate one.

A. Some people charge me of misanthropy and accuse me of thinking only of myself: this creates a sense of guilt in me.

R. My dear one, we said, speaking of the necessary qualities, that you must find the daring to go against the current. Let people talk and say what they will, but you must find the courage to pick up all your strength and go straight ahead along the road you have chosen. Beware, above all, of those whom we might call sentimentalists and of certain kind, of intellectuals who propose to you the problem of extroversion, unselfishness, of good deeds and the like. These people, if we observe their unconscious motives, are deeply selfish and serve nobody but themselves. The first category is unable to stay still and goes about interfering with other people's business; with the excuse of being useful they gratify their own particular need for pleasure. As their satchel is empty they have nothing to offer. They are the usual blind who wish to lead the blind. The others rely on and live off their 'clients'. What would a politician, a certain kind of scholar, a religious fanatic, a speaker do without an audience? A genius, of any order or degree, aims only at 'creating', at bringing into manifestation ideas that exist at the unconscious level, he aims at finding the solution to the 'problem', be it scientific, philosophical, poetical, etc. A great artist creates and that is all; often does not even he know what has emerged from his intuition.

In the various fields there are two kinds of people who adopt this attitude: the first feels instinctively the unconscious expectations of the masses and addresses them, drawing, obviously, advantage from the situation; the other dedicates himself only to discovering the universal Truth and revealing it.

The first kind, addressing the subconsciousness of the masses, cannot represent the light and the direction towards which the masses should direct themselves; the second is the revealer of the supraconscious Truth and therefore the only true light able to guide and comprehend. They say that the genius is always a precursor and ahead of time because his ideas do not in fact belong to his particular time or rather, they are not the same as those currently expressed by the people. As you can see, the former adjusts himself and meets the instinctive desire of the masses while the latter transcends the view of the masses. But every expansion of consciousness has come about thanks to the great geniuses in all fields of cultural expression who, going against the stream and raising themselves above the common crowd, pointed out a new and vaster horizon. Therefore shun like the plague those people who, empty-handed want to give, loveless want to love, without intellect want to enlighten.

Nearly all *yogins* have shut themselves away in all solitude, meditating, persevering in their *sādhanā* and when, eventually, they found themselves covered with treasures, then they have emerged from their condition to give what they had achieved with great difficulty. Remember this, my dear one, the Harmony of the entire world depends upon your inner Harmony. If you realize pure inner Beauty, matter around you will also be turned into Beauty. The perfection of your environment depends upon the perfection of your heart.

A. I understand what you are saying and I am convinced. And yet, especially nowadays, all the so called illuminated persons speak of nothing but activism for the benefit of others, of commitment in order to solve the problems of others and so on.

R. Only to dominate and despise them in the end. Political, financial, etc. groups do nothing but contend the masses, try to win their approval. In the past there have been dictatorships which repressed people through *physical force*, today the democratic or popular dictatorships dominate their followers through *psychological* means, and this is extremely dangerous and diabolical.

You must emerge from what psychology calls collective subconsciousness and, spreading your wings, take to the sky towards the highest peaks of Knowledge. There are many who struggle in order to change the social 'structures'. You instead must try to transform people's consciousness, but you cannot do so until your own consciousness is transformed.

A. Perhaps these attitudes are the outcome of our way of seeing things; in other words we in the West think that reality must always be external to us and although we may recognize this to be untrue, we nonetheless feel unconsciously inclined to part with our centrality.

14

JUNG AND WESTERN EXTROVERSION

R. With regard to this point some of C.G. Jung's statements are really interesting. In his introduction to *The Tibetan Book of the Great Liberation* (Oxford University Press, London), he argues that: "Introversion is, if one may say so, the way of the East, it is the normal, generalized attitude just as extroversion is the way of the West. Here introversion is considered abnormal, pathological.... In the East, however, our beloved extroversion is despised as an illusory desire, as existence within *saṃsāra*, the very essence of the intermingling with the *nidāna* which culminates in the suffering of the worlds.... For those who have even only a rough knowledge of the history of European philosophy, the heated discussion regarding the *universals* which started with Plato will be an instructive example.

... The Christian West considers Man to be completely dependent upon the grace of God or at least upon the Church seen as the exclusive, divinely sanctioned, earthly instrument of human redemption. The East instead, since it believes in *Self-liberation*, insists upon the fact that Man is the only cause of his own emancipation.

... The West, in any case, is entirely Christian as far as its psychology is concerned. Tertullianus's *anima naturaliter christiana* is held to be applicable to the entire West, not in the religious sense—as the author meant in his day—but only in the psychological sense. Grace comes from other places, in any case from without.

... For him (the Westerner) Man is small within, he is almost a nothing and furthermore, as Kierkegaard says, "before God man is always in error".

Through fears, repentances, promises, submissions, self-humiliation, good deeds and praises he propitiates the great power, which is not his self, but *totaliter alter*, altogether Other, totally perfect and *external*, the sole reality.

If one changes the formula a little and substitutes God with some other power, the world for instance, or money, one gets a complete picture of the Western man—diligent, fearful, devout, who humiliates himself and is enterprising, avid and violent in his aspiring to this world's goods: wealth, health, knowledge, technical ability, public welfare, political power, conquest and so on. And what is the meaning of the great popular movements of our day? Attempts at taking possession of the money or of the property of others while defending one's own. The mind is used above all to coin 'isms' which can ably hide the true motives that spur us to obtain greater advantages''.

* * *

A. I take up again our dialogue interrupted by circumstances beyond my control. There have been certain *karmic* adjustments that if on the one side have caused suffering to my individuality, on the other they have left it freer. I find my thirst for Liberation greatly increased, and I must admit that for me now there is only one direction.

Today I can safely state that I am prepared to face anything in order to find myself, in order to emerge from the restrictions of my incompleteness. I have understood too much to go back, too little to be truly free.

I would like to tell you about certain experiences I have had in this period and which I believe to be interesting. I realize that I must open myself completely to you.

R. Your experiences are rather meaningful and this makes me realize that your inner fire is beginning to move along pre-established lines. At this point you can accelerate your *sādhanā*: you have now freed yourself from certain *karmic* relationships, you have overcome every sense of guilt, you are no longer influenced by collective subconscious stimulations, and the 'solitude' of the disciple lives in you. Even though you have had another drug experience, I believe it was your last.

For six months you must carry out this type of meditation, following exactly what I tell you. Every fifteen days you shall report to me about all you have experienced. Besides you shall tell me all the dreams you have.

15

SĀDHANĀ

A. Here I am to give you an account of my *sādhanā.* I have drawn up a synthetic picture of all we have said and I have kept it firm in my heart. It represents my 'vision'. It is easy for me to permeate my heart with the vision, at times I seem to be that very vision.

My imagination is not yet vivid enough and strong enough to move those energies you spoke to me about. However I have realized that the force of thought is great indeed, and this is already something.

I have already done something with regard to my diet, but I proceed with intelligence; I shall use a gradual approach, just as I did with drugs.

Over the past few days I have been hunted by a thought: if the Self is already realized, then who is striving for realization? What do we exactly mean by the term realization?

R. Indeed completeness cannot be looking for completeness; so, for example, the sun-fire cannot be looking for fire. How can we realize or make absolute that which is already absolute?

All we can do is to try and eliminate the false conception (*avidyā*) that we are our ego, with all its perishable and conflicting attributes.

A. But how can the ego, which is incompleteness, recognize or be completeness?

R. The ego with its expressions is not reality but simply a reflection of light and shade, it is *māyā*; thus it is obvious that the non-real is unable to recognize or be reality. So, that *jīva*-self acting in dreams, not being an absolute reality but a shadow projection, cannot realize itself as a reality. We can say that reality reveals itself by itself the very moment in which the ego dies, disappears, just as knowledge does when ignorance is transcended. *Māyā* is an actual fact which is beyond all explanation; it just appears and disappears.

We have to recognize through intuition, as well as by logical rational inference, that behind the ego-shadow there is a reality always identical to itself which, being essential and noumenal knowledge, breaks in upon the world of appearances; *māyā* is a *continuum-discontinuum* which can be interrupted at any moment.

A supraconscious intuition is a ray of knowledge of the Self and not of the ego. For example, the sense of immortality does not come from the body, which is corruptible and therefore unable to give us the idea of eternity, but from the deeper strata of our essence.

The intuition or illumination of the Self makes us understand that the only reality is the Self, and all we have to do is adhering to that which is Reality-Absolute.

All the ego's conceptualizings, all its elaborate theories, its flights, its quantitative erudition never lead us to reality, but only to non-reality. *Māyā* produces only *māyā* and *avidyā*. Therefore, Realization means adhering with total awareness to that intuition which brings about the recognition that we are the Self. And Realization is different from erudition because, while the latter is mere notionism about something, Realization involves *being* that thing.

A. If I understand properly, total Reality is behind the world of appearances just as the atomic nucleus is behind electrons; indeed, it is the very presence of reality that makes possible for the appearances to objectivate themselves. The consciousness of the individual can grasp this ray of Reality eventually realizing a full identity with it. Am I right?

R. Yes, you are quite right. Now, there are three aspects with which you will have to work, as well as others which are consequential to the very process of realization.

The first is intuitive discrimination which separates Being from non-being, what *is* from what is not, truth from error.

The second is detachment, disidentification and 'loosening the grip' concerning what is, in fact, non-being.

The third is finding the right attitude of consciousness so that the radiant fire of the Self may permeate you. In this way you shall render yourself insensible to non-being and open to Being. It is the proper application of repulsion and attraction, of rejection and acceptance. As you become aware of your reality, the shadow-projection dissolves completely, just as thought disappears as the mind becomes aware of what it is.

A. I wish to pose this philosophical question. When I deny a thing, negation itself makes me accept that very thing. By rejecting non-existence I really assert its existence. Thus we are faced with two realities: that of Being and that of non-being.

R. My dear, I think that we have already discussed this issue. Certain pseudo-truths and mental patterns die hard. Let us take up the question again.

First of all we must establish that our research of reality is to be undertaken from the existential point in which we actually are. This implies the acceptance of our system of co-ordinates and from this point we can begin to analyse the problem. The analysis leads us to recognize the fact that this system of co-ordinates is not an absolute, but a simple phenomenal relative and that when compared to other systems of co-ordinates it has but very little significance—it represents only a certain degree of truth—and when compared to others still it disappeas completely. Thus, it is only from the point of view of the Absolute *Brahman* that we can say that the world of names and forms, of any order or degree whatsoever, is just *māyā*. You should also bear in mind that the phenomenal *māyika* world is not non-existent like the hare's horns or the son of a barren woman; it has its own degree of truth, but when compared with another order of truth it loses all its intrinsic significance and, let me repeat it, before other systems of co-ordinates it disappears altogether. A mirage, though being a mirage, has its own type of truth, just as the dream of a person asleep has one. Here lies the mystery of *māyā*: it is and yet it is not, and for *Vedānta* to look for the cause of what is and is not means being all the while conditioned by *māyā*.

Therefore, *Asparśa* does not negate the world of names and forms, but it assigns to it its proper place in the context of things.

A. I understand all this perfectly, unfortunately my subconsciousness still creates me some problems. I realize that man's plight is that of considering a certain order of relative truth as absolute; he truly takes the rope for a snake. On the other hand if he manages to understand that behind this phantasmagoria of names and forms the reality of his being exists he cannot but let go of what he erroneously believed to be the truth. I think that if there are philosophical systems that lead to conflict and pain these are in fact the materialistic systems, that is those which consider as absolute only the formal or tridimensional order of co-ordinates.

R. I am convinced of this myself. The paradox lies in the fact that some philosophies, of a well defined socio-economic order, point out to man the solution to his conflicts and anguish by offering him the tangible 'golden calf', but these are precisely the philosophies that tie down the individual's consciousness, sinking it in conflicts and anguish without end as well as leading it down a blind alley. By materialism I mean that conception which postulates reality outside oneself and on the mere tridimensional sphere; in other words, this conception takes into consideration only a portion (in this case *Virāṭ*: the gross world) of total truth.

16

THE ORIGIN OF THE SUBCONSCIOUSNESS

A. You have spoken of the subconsciousness and of persistent ideas. Why am I forced to think what I do not wish to think? Why do things that no longer have any sense for me keep coming back into my mind? Can you give me an explanation for all this? I feel I need an explanation.

R. I understand. You have said to me in the past that, though your consciousness no longer wished to experience drugs and other things, yet some kind of power pushed you to move towards them; your mind, then, would arrange the experience and predispose the means suitable for carrying it out. How is thought born? Why do we think?

A. Even though I have understood many things, this particular problem escapes me.

R. I believe so too. Let us try to understand something about it. For example, why did you *think* of drugs?

A. Because I was down in the dumps. I was dissatisfied with everything and a friend of mine told me that I needed something exciting, exhilarating...

R. We can add imprisoning and non-resolving. Is that not true?

A. Today I can say so, an absurd exaltation. Too great a price to pay, from every point of view, for the illusion of a moment.

R. Very well, you thought of drugs because compelled by great *dissatisfaction* which pre-existed the drug-idea. Dissatisfaction, lack of gratification, restlessness, which at the unconscious level are indeterminate and not as yet qualified.

A. Thought, I would like to ask, is it not the mind? And where is the subconsciousness? All these terms, along with their location, are incomprehensible to me.

R. Right. Analysis separates and divides what is really one. But you oblige me to make use of analysis. Let us make a comparison. Let us compare the mind to the ocean. The ocean is a particular substance which produces waves, ice, etc. Thus, the mind is a certain type of substance imbued with awareness, will, intelligence, etc., capable of producing certain things, for example, an idea-image. Since a subconscious content is just a coagulated, crystallized idea-event, we may compare it to a piece of ice which is crystallized water.

The association of ideas is like the continuous ebb and flow of the ocean, one wave follows upon another motivated by subconscious stimulations. Memory is a fact, an idea, an image which has left a furrow in the mental substance. Thus we have the following sequence: subconscious request, emotional movement, ideation and conceptualization of the movement-request, action.

The request, or the unconscious germinal thrust, may produce attractive or repulsive movement. From its unconscious and indeterminate condition it slowly emerges, qualifying and objectivating itself.

A. Thus my request for sensory pleasure derives from an unconscious need. Is my request for drugs, for example, due to unconscious urges? However, the first time I used them that urge could not possibly have been there in the unconscious.

R. There was a time when your mind was *free* from such content, but not from the feeling of dissatisfaction. One fine day, or rather, one bad day, a stimulus struck your mind and, as it was already *predisposed*, it promptly accepted the message; in other words, your mind reacted upon it. What happened then? The pleasure experienced was so strong that it left a furrow in the mental substance and set roots there. After some time the memory, sprouting from the root, surfaced again and spurred the mental imagination to project the event. When the entire field of consciousness is covered completely by the mental image there is no way out, the precipitation at the objective level is unavoidable. As a consequence of the repetition of the event the root produces a seed, a small, conditioning atom-force; at this point the experience becomes crystallized concretely in the depths of the mind.

So, in your psychic space there was a nucleus-force able to cyclically oblige you to perform the emotional action and the image-thought. Your mind was compelled to think of the object of its conditioning, it did not experience any idea-image other than that implanted and impressed in its structure. What can we deduce from all this? That the mind, once *free* from the thought of drugs, gradually slipped into a state of *necessity* and of bondage.

This process occurs also with sex, with vanity, with self-assertion, with hate etc., all drugs that dull and blunt the being's awareness.

A. This consoles me. We are all more or less addicted to drugs. Some take a kind of drugs, others another. I realize that we are the children of necessity because we have lost control of our self-determination.

R. That is exactly as things stand. Humanity is drugged and is not aware of it. It lives under the sway of the *affirmation* of hate, of sensual love, of self-assertion, of power and other drugs that offend reason and intelligence.

A. Now I would like to ask you: why does dissatisfaction, which induces us to experience incompleteness, exist?

R. When, as a result of free will, one 'leaves' one's own nature and identifies with one's 'shadows', unless and until one goes back or *awakens* from the stupor of identification one lives in a state of dissatisfaction. But this is healthy since it urges our consciousness, identified with a shadow, to look for its completeness.

For a long time it seeks the object of its completeness outside of itself (hence all the gratifications we have spoken about), but in the end it is left with no alternative but to surrender and retire into itself: the moment of return and withdrawing has come. Then it realizes that all those gratifications were only mere compensations. The ego itself arises as a compensatory event and this is why it can never satiate itself.

Egoism is the law of the ego, it represents the law of its survival. The ego is eagerly looking for *concepts, affections*, and *instincts* because it must compensate for its lack of absoluteness and reality; it has to fight its caducity. It attaches itself to objects because it hopes to find in things-events its perpetuity and its happiness.

The world you see before you is the world of the ego, but your Reality is not of this world. In the world of the ego you can never find completeness or a solution to your basic problems; I can tell you that no socio-economic-political ideology can ever solve the problem of the ego.

The ego has a sole inevitable destiny: that of dying. But it is by this very death that Reality springs forth and gushes like a fountain of immortal life.

A. It is a natural occurrence that when we have no natural products we replace them with artificial ones; we compensate for the loss of certain pure products by availing of artificial ones. Is this also the case as far as we ourselves are concerned?

R. Your practical example fits. Having lost Bliss without objects, we put objective sensory bliss in its place. Having lost principial-universal Knowledge we put mass erudition of phenomena in its place, and so on.

We live on 'surrogates', on 'substitutes', on compensation and alienation.

A. But, having had bliss without object, I ask myself, why on earth have I got tangled up in conflict and pain? Having had the pure product close at hand, why on earth did I have recourse to surrogates?

R. If you have fallen into this it means that you were able to. Let us say that your *nature* is such that you can experience infinite possibilities of life.

Let us try to understand what happens at mental-*manasic* level. You have the possibility and the freedom to think all you wish, within the sphere of your nature obviously. Now pay attention: you may think and remain free from your thoughts, or else you may think and merge yourself with your objective thought to the point where you no longer consider yourself a thinking subject but an object of thought.

Do we agree on this point?

A. Certainly. Looking back over my experiences I can safely say so.

R. Well, remember then that all this is part of your nature, of your being. If you are unable to modify the conceptual framework which you have of the *nature* of a thing, you may fall into great conflicts.

If your restless mind should ask, for example, why you are a male and not a female, why a human and not something else, I should tell you that you are going against a principle of rational logic; you are a male because such is your nature; *you are what you are*, that is all. We cannot discuss the nature of a thing because, in fact, it is what it is; however we can discuss about the workings of that particular kind of nature, how it operates and determines itself. *Manas* is a vehicle of investigation which, besides having by necessity certain limitations, must recognize the fact that there are certain 'whys' that have no answer for the simple reason that these 'whys' belong to the very *nature* of being. We may say that there are ultimate realities that are such precisely because they are ultimate.

A. I understand. The fault does not lie in truth or in things because, as you say, they are what they are; the fault lies in the wrong mental direction. The *manas*-mind is a simple vehicle of investigation and if there is no awareness behind it which tells you to beware not to go down a blind alley, then you will go on asking the impossible.

R. I agree. Therefore, do not ask yourself, as far as the mind itself is concerned, why it thinks; the mind thinks because it is its nature to think; just as we know that dampness is connatural to water, and so on.

Getting back to our topic we can conclude by saying that you can easily see—without the need of any dialectical demonstration—that you are free to think without identifying yourself with the product of thought, just as you can think and identify with it; and, we can now add, you are even free not to think at all.

We have, therefore, three ways in which the mind can operate:

1. Thinking with identification
2. Thinking without identification
3. Not thinking.

The first condition is that of the vast majority of living beings, whence comes the loss of one's own identity and as a consequence the acquisition of all those surrogates which we spoke about earlier.

The second condition is that of the realized one at the ontological level (if such an expression can be allowed); the third is that of him who has transcended both the *need to do* with identification and of *acting* without discernment.

A. But is the mind not solicited by external stimuli which condition us apart from internal unconscious ones?

R. That is right. It is affected also by external agents. The water of the ocean can be put in motion by the icebergs it harbours or by the impulse-stimulation produced by an external factor.

A. Therefore, as long as there are stimulations or solicitations from without we are obliged to produce thought and therefore mind-consciousness modifications. This is a kind of bondage we are unable to fight.

R. We must recognize the fact that our mind-consciousness, if it really wants to, though solicited by external agents can remain unmodified, can establish itself as a central point without any emotional reaction or production of images. How many times have you received stimulations from outside without actually modifying your mind-consciousness? This has the possibility of setting itself in a *neutral* position.

A. All we have said is of great importance, to me at least. How can I draw up a synthesis of all this so that such a seed of meditation may take root in a permanent way in my mental substance?

R. We can summarize it all in this scheme, which proposes itself cyclically:

Consciential Quietness

↓

1. Original impulse, cause of movement (Solicitation)
2. Qualified emotional movement (Consciousness modification)
3. Imagination and planning of the event with consequent quest for the means suitable to gratify the need and calm the movement.
4. Extinction of the movement

↓

Consciential Quietness

As you can see, between two positions of *quietness*, of calm, of rest, there is tension-modification of consciousness.

One day you will arrive at a particular type of action devoid of this tension-modification, which means that though acting you will be at peace with yourself and therefore with life; it means that you will place yourself outside of the psychic becoming, outside of the conflicting polar movement. I think that you have gathered this when I spoke about the expressions of *manas.* But let us take up our topic again. The impulse is a minimum of potential energy of a seed that is well rooted in the mental substance. The movement is the setting in motion of the emotion-sentiment. It is the psychic tension which urges the mind to ideate and imagine, to organize itself through planning and to modify the consciousness. Movement represents the psychic *māyā*-becoming. The extinction of the movement comes about with the ceasing of the stimulus, with the gratification of the directing content, with the relief of the tension.

A. And if the whole process starts repeating: need, movement, etc., how can we find a way out of this hellish situation?

R. That is true, the repetition is cyclic and constant because the seed takes vigour again, it feeds itelf precisely through repetition, that is to say by assimilating the pleasure-pain or the *quality* of the fact, of the experience, just as the repetition of the muscular movement trains and increases the muscle. The drug of sex, of vanity, etc., or the one you have been taking up to now, causes you pleasure (or pain, which amounts to the same thing).

Pleasure-pain has the power to create a furrow in the mental substance, to cut into it; the consequent compulsory repetition causes further pleasure-pain which provides new food for the seed, and so on. Therefore, the seed can perpetuate indefinitely, nourishing itself by the play of its own vital rhythm. An idea-content is an *entity*, with a vitality of its own; it can exalt you or destroy you. It depends on the potential quality of the entity-seed-idea, it depends on the direction that it takes.

A. What a desolation! Can this enslaving circle ever be broken?

R. Yes it can, fortunately. But preparation, will-power and intelligence are required.

If we bring the whole movement production down to slow-motion, we can see the sequences we mentioned before. Thus we can step in at any given point along the four phases:

- We can, that is, prevent the mind from ideating-imagining and thus not allow it to be involved in the emotional movement. This represents the breaking of the mental image; the mind always works by images.
- We can, by finding an equal and opposite force, halt the movement of the senses. This represents the compression of the sensible-sentimental emotional force.
- We can stop the original impulse of the mental substance before it can arouse the emotional excitement.

This last possibility is the best of conditions because, besides all else, it is not the outcome of inhibition, as we mean it in the normal sense, in that the annulment occurs at a very deep level, outside of the conscious framework.

In other words we descend into 'hell' to root out *in loco* our incompleteness and our dissatisfaction. If we adopt this procedure, we can make use at the same time of the first two as well, because the tension is released gradually; if on the other hand we use only the first two phases, we cannot solve the problem totally because the solution occurs at a far too superficial level of the psyche. I gave you a technique to follow to this end and we shall speak more about it later on.

A. Before leaving I would like to tell you about the dreams that keep recurring during this last period. It has something to do with water. In front of me there are rivers, lakes, sometimes the sea. For instance, I happen suddenly to come across a huge current which prevents me from advancing.

I also find myself on a cliff, in the midst of the current, and I would like to jump back onto the bank but I am afraid and then I wake up.

Another time I even seemed to drown: the water arrived at my throat at which point I woke up.

However I no longer have those grim dreams when I used to find myself underground; I do not dream any more—not at least with that frequency—of steep and violent descents that used to shake me so much that I woke up with a start.

17

TRANSMIGRATION

A. The last time we met I told you that I would have liked to leave the tridimensional framework of co-ordinates and never be reincarnated again. I am more than ever convinced that I have nothing whatsoever to do with the world of *māyā*, with the world of *exaltation* and, therefore, of all psychical and physical drugs.

R. When you speak of reincarnation to what do you refer exactly?

A. To the theory of reincarnation of which we spoke some time ago. Have I not reincarnated in this world of unfulfilment? You have often spoken to me in the sense that I should leave the framework birth-death. Is that not so?

R. We had better take up this question again because I think you have not grasped the essence of the problem. Granted that the Self has neither a birth nor an end and is timeless and uncaused, in what sense and up to what point can we speak of rebirth or, seeing that it is the same thing, of death?

A. Therefore, basing myself on what for me is a recognition, a *constant* if it is such cannot undergo change, and so it is not subject to a modification of nature. A constant cannot have origin because if it had it could not be called infinite and eternal. Death and birth are qualifications inherent in something contingent. The Self is constant, absolute, universally valid, therefore it can neither be born nor die. Who is it then that reincarnates?

R. This is the point: who reincarnates?

A. Some months ago we spoke about an entity called *jīva*. Can we attribute the cause of reincarnation to it? Is it the root of our troubles?

R. In fact it is their cause. The *jīva* is only a name which covers a certain experimental truth. It is the reverberation of the *ātman*-constant.

This 'consciential reverberation' being able to express itself in countless ways, with time acquires particular qualifications which it crystallizes around itself until it becomes enslaved by its very own materialized experiences. For example, the mind, while being able to direct itself towards multiple thoughts, in the long run it crystallizes some of them until it becomes their slave. The children devour their father.

When this consciential reverberation is tied down and imprisoned by the web that it itself has woven, it cannot but follow its qualitative directions. We went into it in detail the other time. Therefore the *jīva*, compelled by certain experiences which it can receive and live, for example on the physical plane, is obliged to follow the way of incarnation on that plane of vital expression, taking possession of the body inherent in it. As you can see, the subconscious tendencies that have not been solved, the *vāsanās*, the *saṃskāras* (subconscious impressions) which, not being transcended, cause this situation, often undesirable, to endure. It is always the *saṃskāras* which oblige the mind to repeat the same line of thought, up to the point of obsession.

A. You said that the *jīva* can manifest itself along countless vital expressions. Can it, therefore, choose to experience a non-human state of consciousness?

R. Quite so. In the universe there are indefinite—though finite—expressions of life, and the *jīva* is free to choose to transmigrate, if it manages to have experience without becoming imprisoned or tied to a specific expression of life. This would be the ideal condition on the plane of *māyika* living.

A. Should it act completely detached from the fruit of its actions?

R. Certainly. For such a *jīva* there would be no accumulation of *karma* because it would not be tied to anything.

R. But you speak of *māyika* living.

R. We must recognize the fact that the *jīva* is only a shadow, a reflection, a non-reality; even though it can live without *karma* still it remains within the limit of its nature and of the nature of the world of names and forms. Although it can express very elevated non-restricting tendencies, like intelligence, love and will of good, it nonetheless remains within the sphere of *māyā-avidyā.*

A. Therefore we can speak of transmigration with reference to these tendencies, needs, qualified energetic directions, can we not?

R. That is so. First of all the term transmigration is more appropriate; then when the desire-tendencies cease, also compulsion, slavery and therefore transmigration of the energy itself come to an end. For *ātman* there is neither *jīva* nor transmigration, just as for the sun there is neither dawn nor sunset.

A. I understand the problem of transmigration better now. The aim is that of dissociating oneself or of resolving the subconsciousness, even the unconscious tendency to think of oneself as a human individual, is that right?

R. Quite so. For *Advaita* not only one must stop considering oneself as a human individual, but one must stop thinking of oneself in terms of any other possible formal life, whether gross or subtle. For *Advaita* there is neither *jīva* nor transmigration.

A. Today I wish to tell you that my physical body and my mind are in the process of achieving a new vibratory rhythm. The things of the external world now appear to me as multiple vibratory states. Once I was afraid of abandoning the supports of profane life, today I realize that my fear was unfounded. There is nothing for which it is worth our while to become attached. But on the other hand it is not a question of abandoning anything; when the entity lives fulfilling consciential aspects it has no further reactions because those profane things lose their fascinating power, those objective systems of co-ordinates become more vague in their outlines, they recede or disappear completely.

I am observing the marvels of my transformation, I am

watching the process of solution of the 'coagulation' I determined in the past. Just a little more *fire* and the energetic coagulation will evaporate into total dispersion.

My dear Brother, your vibrations fill my heart and I feel that they are saying to me: 'to die is beautiful';

> ‹to extinguish the 'fire' of one's own instincts (*solid*), to evaporate the 'water' of one's own emotions (*liquid*) and to dissolve the 'air' of one's own thought (*aeriform*)›

is the task of the person who has posed himself the problem of returning to the Centre. As you can notice, even my language has changed. And this fills me with joy.

18

COMPENSATIONS OF THE EGO

R. As you can see there is an ever more perfect syntony of our hearts. I am beginning to think that gradually we shall understand one another not so much by means of words but through vibratory accord. By realizing Truth *we are* Truth, and Truth demonstrates itself, it reveals itself innocently, it comes forth like the fire of the sun, in the all-pervading silence.

I wish to remind you of something concerning the supports of which you spoke earlier. There are many disciples who have achieved a strong detachment from profane life. They have disciplined themselves on the plane of attraction towards material things, on the plane of their diet, on the plane of their human relations, limiting them to the utmost, and the like. They appear to be realized, and they even thrive on silence. Looking at them one might think that they were 'outside of this world'. However, a closer look reveals to sharper eyes that they have transferred onto the subjective level what before was desire-incentive at the objective level. They have created for themselves an ideal world which answers perfectly to the gratifications of the ego. From being extroverts they have turned into introverts. They have abandoned nothing, they have simply carried out a transfer of energies and of spheres.

Gradually their consciousness adjusts—when it is not its line of least resistance—to this ideal movement and finds in it that gratification which first it found outside of itself. Thus we have dreamers who gratify themselves by means of their own dreams. There are individuals who imagine they be sport champions, actors, politicians, industrialists, religious leaders, teachers, *avatāras* or messiahs, lords of the masses; in brief, important people who always find followers. Sometimes, an altruistic motivation is attributed to all this imagining and this is extremely dangerous and subtle, because the ego-need thus finds the way clear as all this answers to a certain kind of common morality, an ideal situation which can be accepted, welcomed even with complacency. The consciousness is thus set at rest and does not offer any resistance leaving a free way to the egoistic satisfaction. This is a demonstration of great instinctive astuteness on the part of the conditioning energy, a pleasant alibi for the avid and psychically onanist ego.

In order to understand this event you must learn to recognize the mode in which this desire-need operates.

The *vāsanās*, that is the subconscious forces, impel towards needs of pleasure. They spur to 'movement' so as to be gratified. Gratification usually occurs at the objective level, therefore the mind instinctively plans a course of action that will lead to the conclusion of the gratification itself. In this type of situation we find all those people who operate and act in order to determine themselves along countless lines of behaviour; the outcome is, obviously, satisfaction of the desire-need. When this is not gratified, the psyche, insofar as it is a flow of energy 'reaching out for', remains frustrated. This is the condition of the ego in conflict. If, on the other hand, the request is matured and met, there occurs a discharge of tension ('pleasure' is tension) and the consciousness is for a while tranquil, content and pacified. We can say that, after all, the deepest need of the human being is in fact that of reaching a state of tranquillity and peace of mind. We may also say that—and it is a paradox—true peace of heart comes from the death-gratification of desire-pleasure.

The maturation of need-desire implies contraction, restlessness and a-rhythmical movement of the psyche, while the release and death of desire-tension brings a sweet abandonment, a healthy relaxing, a complete reconciliation of the bio-psychic powers. We made some mention of this before. But it is worthwhile going into deeper details.

A. I have experienced this process personally in the fields of drugs and sex. I find that it corresponds with facts. But how can one solve such an event completely and in an integral way?

R. In fact, this is the basic problem if one really wishes to emerge from tension-conflict.

As needs arise, mature and die only to be reborn, mature and die again, and so on cyclically, how can we solve the problem? If we continue to gratify desire-needs we do not solve the problem because until we carry within ourselves the seeds of desire, the very force of life will stimulate them into maturity. As long as the roots of a tree are well planted, the sun will make its fruit ripen regularly. To prevent this from happening we must eliminate either the sun or the favourable environmental conditions. However, although the favouring conditions may be absent, the root seeds will always remain ready to shoot forth into development and maturation.

A. If I am not mistaken this condition corresponds to *pralaya*, is that right?

R. That is right. It corresponds to the 'sleep' of nature. Life remains at a latent state, waiting for a new dawn.

Thus, as long as there are seeds that require gratification one is involved on the plane of becoming and process, and this constitutes the swinging movement of the individual, the movement of the pendulum of a clock.

The *saṃsāric* individual experiences this ebb and flow: calm, tension and gratification followed by calm, and so on. However, there are beings who in time, on reaching maturity, tired of this to-and-fro movement, wish to put an end to it, and so they stop and begin considering a way of escape.

You are at this point. You are meditating and trying to solve this vital ebb and flow, you are applying yourself to the possibility of escaping from this rest-tension framework; in other words, from the flow of the individual and universal becoming.

A. I am convinced of this now. During this period I have understood so many things, I have seen myself, I have experienced, I have analyzed by my awareness and I have arrived at the conclusion that I must solve once and for all this see-saw movement, it is not for me any longer, it is an absurdity, a mere child's game.

R. Therefore you must cut off the cause of desire and conflictual becoming at the root, you must transcend the *fount* of the objective and subjective swinging, and the fount lies—to say it with *Advaita*—in the causal-germinal body. The roots of *avidyā* are planted here, the source of your potential energy that forces you into the ebb-flow movement of pleasure-pain, whether subtle or gross, subjective or objective, dwells in this body. This body, sphere, condition, etc., call it as you will, represents the container of the instinctive *potency*, in a broad sense, which, until it finds a solution, goes on bursting into *act* through some channel or other. And if you close one channel, the pressure of the instinctive potency not gratified will open a new one. We have seen that if we reject a desire, after a while we find ourselves with another desire directed towards something else.

If you wish to resolve the see-saw of becoming, you must reach *Pax Profunda* which is bliss without an object, without desire, without gratification; which is Peace and not a relaxation after the discharge of tension, nor exaltation or sensible ecstasy.

My dear one, *Asparśa-yoga* is the *yoga* without supports, it is the *yoga* which pulls the roots out from their depths, it is the *yoga* of integral solution.

A. I understand perfectly and I daringly push forward in dying to myself. Shall I continue with my meditation and all the rest that I already know?

R. I shall give you another meditation. Give an increasingly more regulated rhythm to your breathing, take in your hands the sword of *viveka* (discrimination between Real and non-real) and of *vairāgya* (psychological detachment) with greater decision and determination. Point your attention towards the *Vision*, and let yourself go to the sweetness of Self. If at times you should see the fleeting fires, put them out and live the joy of the 'last breathings'.

A. If we have no more to say I would like to tell you about my recent dreams. For some time now I dream that I am *flying*, yes, flying. It may seem silly, but it is true. The fact amuses me, really, because I feel a sense of freedom, I feel lighter. At times I see somebody following me and I suddenly take flight;

I alight on trees, on rooftops; sometimes I become tangled up in electric wires. Other times I find it hard to lift off the ground. I move my arms like wings. What a strange sensation! A month or so ago I dreamed I was flying and then I run into a huge cloud, or at least, that is what it seemed like. I could see almost nothing except a dark smoky mass all around me. I was afraid and when I woke up my heart was beating wildly.

19

DYING TO ONESELF

A. I have come back after almost a whole year. *Karmic* reasons kept me away, but I have kept up the *sādhanā* just the same. I wish to ask you this: you gave me techniques and meditations, but is *Asparśa* not beyond all these psycho-physical means? I think we stressed this in the past.

R. This is true. However, your transformation came about more on account of the *understanding* which emerged from our dialogue than any other thing. I have tried to transfuse to you my own awareness, to stimulate those seeds, already on the point of awakening, which were in you. The techniques have only been coadjuvants, they are 'devices' that operate in your spatiality and I use them only for certain purposes.

A. Do they allow me to conquer the Self in a shorter time?

R. For some people these techniques are of great help. But what annuls time is watchfulness. Only he who is watchful saves himself.

The *Dhammapada* (*sūtra* 30) says: "Through watchfulness, Maghavā (the God Indra) achieved supreme Lordship over the Gods".

Watchfulness is total self-awareness, it is complete openness; as long as there is watchfulness there are no impediments or obstacles within our psychic spatiality. Whosover is watchful is outside of time.

I believe you have talked of *conquering* the Self, but in truth you do not have to conquer it. The Self is not conquered, not grasped, not held.

A. What shall I do, then? My consciousness is longing for the Infinite now.

R. You have only 'to die'; in *your* death you will find true *life without illusions.* Self reveals itself as you from 'mass' resolve yourself into 'energy'.

A. Now I understand better. It is what I am actually doing. In any case, I have dreamed of being dead or about to enter a coffin. The other night I dreamed of things like this and I was truly shaken. The experience was more vivid than I could have at the waking state.

I dreamed that you were on an island, on top of a mountain; all around was water so clear as to reflect the beauty of a rainbow. I was at the mouth of a tunnel and at the other end of it I could see an open coffin and an individual dressed in blue with a great sword in his hands. I realized that if I wanted to reach you I had to go down the tunnel and be beheaded. That man was there for this purpose. On the other hand I had no choice, this was the only way. I was taken by such an anguish—increased by the fact that I could not come to you—that I awoke. Even when awake I could still see the scene; I was almost frightened.

R. What you say is very interesting. I can wait.

A. You are smiling and, right now, so am I. This matter no longer worries me, however I must recognize the fact that there are still some small resistances. If this had happened at the beginning of our dialogue I am sure I would not be here today.

R. Remember that everything happens at the right time. As you can see, the event you fear does not happen, even today. You have said yourself that when the consciousness is mature one does not have to abandon anything; the things of the world lose all worth and all meaning.

Whosoever travels down the Way of return, every event will present itself to him at the right moment. The disciple need not worry about anything except maturing his understanding.

A. When I am here I seem to be the Self already and to have overcome all these things which, I recognize, belong after all to the problems of the illusory ego.

R. Well said. They are things that belong to the ego and it is the ego that worries about them. To die to the ego is not an easy thing, but the ego must know that sooner or later it has to resolve itself. Whoever is born and grows, cannot but have a death, an end. For me your ego is already dead.

A. I wish I could think so too; however this comforts me and gives me courage. If I think of all the countless pains and conflicts that it has given me I feel like putting an end to it at once.

R. The ego wanders through the great ocean of *saṃsāra* in search of pleasure, but pleasure is connected with pain in an indissoluble way. Pleasure-pain is a coin with two faces. Where there is one the other is there too. To try to isolate pleasure from pain is an impossible task, and yet man has been trying to do so for millions of years, without success, however. Let us say that he wants to fight a battle lost right from the start. As his initial consciential position is wrong all the consequences are equally wrong. The individual is always a prey to compensations, to retreats and compromises because he cannot find himself outside of the frame of reference of pleasure-pain. His mind is tossed from one pole to the other, like the pendulum of a clockwork, without knowing how to escape. It is a veritable folly.

A. Today I understand fully what you say and, thanks to you, I am happy I can leave all that behind. I think that if others could learn about this resolutive way out they too could follow it. Where is the madman who, having learnt where a treasure is situated, does not set out to possess it?

R. My dear one, do not be amazed. Many know where to look for the treasure but, because they are in fact mad, they do not wish to move. Humanity had never been abandoned, never left an orphan. However do not deceive yourself, the death of the ego and of its incompleteness is not for the many; the solution of the problem of pleasure-pain, of the see-saw of the senses and all other possible forms of duality is not for all, although everyone, sooner or later will come to a dead end and be obliged to stop and think about what to do.

A. I am at least happy that there are many spiritualists who are looking for the treasure.

R. My dear, there are many who speak of spirituality, but very few speak of the 'death of the ego', and fewer still who do not speak at all about it because they are intent upon their own sacrifice. He who is carrying the *Work* to its completion does not cry out, he requires silence.

A. I think that this consideration of yours is somewhat harsh. Do not you think so?

R. It is not I who say these things, though I agree with them, but Buddha, Śaṃkara and all the true Realized ones. Christ himself speaks of the 'narrow gate'. The truth is never hard. It is the ego that considers it so; and often the ego is in search of those spiritual, political, revolutionary *gurus*, etc. who, whether in good or bad faith, promise easy earthly or heavenly paradises or *nirvāṇas*, according, of course, to the philosophical outlook of the *guru*.

You yourself have been able to verify that in order to pull off even a tiny part of incompleteness you have to leave behind shreds of flesh.

A. I realize more and more what good luck I have had. I do not regret anything from my past. I am happy to be near you and that you are teaching me the 'art of dying'. I should not have wished to find myself among those who speak only of esoterism, of spiritualism, of magic and of traditional historicism.

However I am saddened at seeing so many people suffering needlessly. I wish so much to act.

R. Have we not said that you must emerge from the framework of pleasure-pain bouncing?

A. But you must admit that Buddha and Christ showed great compassion and love. They acted.

R. Certainly, I agree with you. Only, that kind of Love and Compassion is different, very different from what you are feeling at the moment. Yours is the fruit of egoistic sentimentality which, however noble, is not worthy of a person who is in flight towards the sphere of no supports. In order to do something really useful in the world one must first leave the world. If you wish to illuminate those who are in ignorance, you must first emerge from ignorance.

A. You tell me things that by intuition alone I feel do not belong to this earth. I realize that I must transcend both my and the collective subconsciousness. On the other hand, in the past we have spoken about it. The fact is that I force myself not to act; I see, I consider, I am sorry for the others and yet I do not act. But you are acting with me and with others, why then should I not act?

R. I do not tell you not to love, not to have compassion and not to act. My action is different from what you would be able to do *today*.

I am never sorry about anything, nor do I see the world the way you see it, or make dualistic and sentimental considerations. My acting is not acting as you mean it; I might even tell you that though acting I do not act because there is no ego in me that can act, feel, consider, compare, be moved and anguished. There is no ego that can tie itself down to anything, even to *Advaita Vedānta* or to *Asparśa-yoga* the basic principles of which I revealed to you.

A. At times I get the idea that the great Beings are continually grieved by the sufferings of men.

R. The 'Gods' do not cry over the sufferings of men, nor over their death. Birth and death, suffering and happiness, good and evil exist only in the world of *māyā*.

A. And what do they spend their time on?

R. Certainly not in gossip, in weeping, in anxiety or in improper exultation which is all a waste of time, but they use their lives by giving their Harmony innocently to space.

When a flower effuses its perfume it does not carry out any action; the perfume is simply the irradiation of its nature.

My dear one, in a world full of pain there is no time to feel sorry or to cry about oneself or others.

A. I have the vague sensation that commiseration and pity are but weaknesses of the ego.

You have told me so many things that I have to stop and put some order in my mind. There are certain points that need further clarification.

20

BEING IN THE WORLD BUT NOT OF THE WORLD

A. I return with a much clearer mind and my attitude is one of profound receptiveness. Some time ago you told me that you do not see the world as I see it. What do you mean?

R. Yes, I remember. In fact, your world is not mine.

A. And yet we are in the same world and perceive the same things.

R. I may be in the world but my consciousness does not belong to it, I may have nothing to do with it.

A. But you perceive it.

R. No, I do not perceive it. I do not see what you see.

A. I wish to clarify this point better. There is something wrong or something I cannot understand...

R. You see the snake, I see the rope. That's all. Śaṃkara often makes use of the example of the snake superimposed on the rope.

Walking along a country lane, we happen to see a snake, but at a closer examination we see that it is a simple piece of rope. What have we done? We have superimposed the image of a snake upon the rope-reality. The snake is the world of names and forms, the world of multiplicity superimposed upon the substratum-constant which is the ultimate Reality of things.

A. I apologize for insisting, but if you live in this world how can you avoid seeing it?

R. The rope is not outside of this world, in fact the rope is what you call the world. The snake, after all, is nothing but the rope itself, that is *Brahman*. You see by the eyes of *māyā* and so you see what really is not there, or you perceive the rope as a snake. Whoever lives Reality cannot see non-reality. He cannot see illusory shapes and fleeting phenomena. Do you not agree?

A. I am deeply attentive. I am compenetrating in the state of your consciousness. It is a well established fact that if I wish to emerge from certain frames of reference I cannot expect to see things as before. I am trying hard to recognize the position of consciousness of the one who is outside of *saṃsāric* becoming, outside of *māyika* universal ebb and flow.

R. I agree. You should not therefore be amazed at certain statements I make, nor cling to your mental co-ordinates otherwise you will not be able to escape them.

A. The other time you said that you love, feel compassion and produce actions, but that you do not love and act in this world and for the others. If you do not see this world as I see it, I ask myself, why do you move and towards whom, seeing that for you all the others are 'snakes' (non-real data)?

R. First, I remember telling you that my actions, my love and my compassion are of a different order than those of yours; and I gave you the example of the flower's perfume. And then, it is not I who see the others as snakes, it is you. I see the others as *Brahman*-rope. For me *Brahman* is everything, and there is nothing apart from *Brahman*.

A. Can you tell me how you see me who am here right in front of you? I might even dare to ask: do you see me?

R. How cannot I see you if you are myself? Or rather, to tell you the truth, I do not see you precisely because you are myself; what could I see outside of myself? What could I perceive outside of Unity?

A. I am realizing something. For some time now you have been taking away from me certain conceptual supports. The objective, external or profane ones have already disappeared, but I realize that I am still living with a number of ideal ones, of thought. Now you are putting me on the edge of the abyss.

Although it is I who am putting myself in these conditions, I ask myself why you are doing such a patient work with me.

R. Whys belong to a mind which has not understood.

A. I can understand this much. What solution do you suggest to the problem?

R. When the abyss is crossed, problems are not solved the way you think they should, they simply disappear. When the cause giving rise to the problem is eliminated, no problem exists any longer. For example, the problem of the cure concerns the sick person but the healthy person does not concern himself with cures or the like. There is not even the incentive for raising the problem.

A. In the Unity you have spoken about are there no others?

R. In Unity there are no *others*. Unity is Unity, not multiplicity, it is Quintessence. Remember of when we spoke of the cube, the tetrahedron and the parallelepiped.

A. I remember, but today I find myself in a different condition; then, for obvious reasons, there was only understanding of concepts, now there is the assimilation of a deep consciential position; this is why I come back to certain themes. I am deeply intent at grasping your state of being which is indeed also mine. On the other hand I realize that the mental support is in my way. So, whoever lives Unity does not pose himself any existential problem, is that right?

R. Existential problems concern the maturation of need-*qualifications* relevant to the *jīva*-shadow; do we agree on this point?

A. Certainly. Illness concerns whoever has a body, and happiness is relevant to the sensible state of the individual.

R. Very well. So, every *jīva* expresses qualifications: it hears, perceives, experiences hate, love, thirst for power, quantitative knowledge and so on. In a word: the *jīva* expresses itself according to the laws of its being. Similarly, the element iron has qualifications of hardness, heaviness, colour, etc. But when the *jīva*—through resolving knowledge or knoweldge by Identity—disappears, of what qualifications can we speak? When the iron-mass resolves itself into energy, all its qualifications disappear, and from necessity it attains to Liberty.

A. I understand why you do not express yourself with the qualifications common to the other *jīvas.* However you too have a body. How do you see it and what relationships have you with it?

R. I see it as you might see an image on a screen at the cinema. What relationship could I entertain with mere non-real image?

A. At this point I am beginning to collapse. I am living on the support of a mental representation, continued for thousands of years, which conceives of the body as a real and substantial thing.

R. Do you admit that the body is a 'coming-and-going', therefore a fleeting appearance? Do you admit that you are something more than a simple 'coming-and-going'?

A. Intellectually I agree, but the consequent mechanism by which the concept becomes consciousness fails to click.

R. You yourself are consciousness. You do not have to ask permission of anyone to live a consciential state. You are the screen and you are the light that makes the images appear on the screen. You have the possibility of coagulating and dissolving, of fixing and loosening.

A. You see, in this moment my subconsciousness would appreciate some comfort, a little relief, but you nail me to the spot, instead.

R. My dear one, I understand you fully and I realize that your ego is looking for compensation, but we are here to dare and to be inflamed by the sacred ardour to cross the abyss. Do you not think so? I am convinced that you are a seeker capable of daring.

A. Certainly. Reality belongs to those who dare. There are moments of bewilderment, unfortunately, and the vision becomes blurred.

R. You have mentioned the subconsciousness before. I think that the key to your problem is right in this very word: subconsciousness. *Vedānta*, as we have seen in the past, speaks of *vāsanās* and of *saṃskāras*: crystallized ideas. The 'monster' you have to destroy is this crystallized world, old and *coagulated.* In any case, we have to admit that you have driven several blows to your 'monster', and your *sādhanā* has pushed ahead considerably.

In the past we spoke of death. It is not that you must die physically—it would be far easier—what you must do, instead, is: obtain the death of the coagulated *idea* that you are a snake and not the rope, that you are a body, senses, etc. and not *That*, the ever shining *ātman*, the One-without-a-second, the Quintessence of all possible quintessence.

A. At times I seem to find myself already in the ultimate Truth, other times, instead, Truth seems to be so far away. There are times when I believe the individual is merely playing with himself or fooling himself; it would be sufficient to put an end to the game and all would return to its proper place.

From now on I must refuse the idea of being this or that, I must refuse every idea of differentiation. I may go crazy, but I will not allow the idea-monster to enter my consciousness.

R. I agree with this decision and I am sure that sooner or later you will obtain what you now impose on yourself. Some time ago you said you wanted to leave all childish games behind you. In any case it is not a question of refusing or of opposing your subconsciousness. You must *comprehend* your subconscious movement, you have to realize that a ball to which an impulse has been applied has its own trajectory, and its force of inertia makes it go on even when the impulse is no longer applied. The important thing for you, now, is not to aliment or give impulse to that idea-monster, otherwise you will create for yourself a great conflict.

A. What can I do? The idea-monster is always present. Strong measures are required.

R. Once I spoke to you of watchfulness, now is the time to really take it into consideration, nay, to live it out.

Watchfulness will lead you gradually to silence, to the suspension of all conscious or unconscious thought modifications. In that silence you will find death and in that same silence you will *discover* yourself once again as Essence.

A. What actions do you advise me to perform when I am realized?

R. When you will be in that state you will not need any suggestions at all, and neither will you have any doubt as to the manner in which to act. Whoever *is* reveals himself naturally, innocently, without any emotional-mental problems of reference.

A. In my present situation then, what do you advise me to do besides my *sādhanā* duties?

R. You should, as we said the other day, compenetrate yourself more and more with the idea of being *That, Brahman*, the Essence of all things, the screen upon which the chiaroscuros of phenomenal life play. Surrender to such awareness, do not oppose the Reality that is in you, lay down all mental, emotional and reactive-physical burden and live the joy of non-resistance. One arrives at Freedom by dominating and transcending the *need* of moving.

A. At times I have faith, at times I need the demonstration, at even other times there is a consciousness void that forces me into inertia.

R. You must gradually substitute faith and intellectual demonstration with inner experience. There are many who travel upon the wings of faith, others on those of mental demonstration; you on the other hand must *live* the truth not by faith or demonstration but because you can accomplish a total revolution of consciousness, because you have achieved that Dignity that grants superior stature. Yours must be Realization, not conceptualization or a simple belief through faith. Remember that the mind goes looking for theories, emotions, sensations, and the ego for gratifications.

A. At the beginning of our dialogue did not we speak of theories, in our case in particular of *Vedānta* theories? Why did we feed the mind with something that has no sense?

R. *Vedānta* is not a theory but a Doctrine, which is not the fruit of intellectual speculation aimed at gratifying the mind in its play. *Vedānta,* rather than speculation, is above all experimentation. From that experimentation arises a conceptualization which concerns only those who have not yet awakened. In other words this means bringing consciential experience onto the plane of verbal communication, the only one open to the non-awakened. An *Upaniṣad* is not a conceptualized theory with no other purpose, but a vision of life translated into concepts which, let us repeat it, are the only medium accessible to the non-awakened. *Brahman* is merely a name that, of course, hides Reality which has no name. Instead of *Brahman* we may use another name—*That* is often used, precisely in order to reduce language to a minimum—but the result does not change. Thus, the idea-*Īśvara* incorporates a precise copsciential experience which we can give any name we wish, but it remains in any case a state of being. To communicate at our level we need language, but the *Upaniṣad* says that *Brahman* is beyond name and language.

Gradually we have abandoned the relationship between two minds (*manas*) to step upon the plane of experimentation. A revolution of consciousness cannot take on simple conceptual bases.

A. You have the gift of giving me peace of heart and other most precious things. I am deeply convinced that the most important fact for Man is *to find* himself again and *to be aware* of himself. I recognize a sole supreme purpose in life: to be *That.* Humanity has but this purpose facing it: to be *That.* The entire manifestation unceasingly longs for and tends towards one sole objective: *That*. Today I can really understand that all men's and Gods' actions, all works, the intellectual, social, moral, etc. needs are nothing but mere expedients that end when one finds *That*. Many consider these means-expedients as the ultimate aim, thus falling into error and conflict. Men can find true peace and true self awareness, true bliss when they embrace *That*.

I consider as false prophets those who try to offer peace and serenity while remaining within the sensible-conflictual dualism and on this infinitesimal objective material part of total Life.

R. *My son*, by the manner in which you express yourself, that revolution of consciousness I spoke to you about is reaching its maturity. I am happy because these your words are not the result of escapes, of compromises, of reactions and the like, but they come of comprehension matured by hammer blows, and achieved by sacrifice, intelligent discrimination and patient reflection.

A. May I conclude our dialogue asking you to meditate with me?

R. Let us meditate.

* * *

A. I am in a state of imponderability; the world of men appears to me out of focus, hazy, very far off; I look around me and I feel like an alien. I ask myself, why on earth am I here?

Nothing creates a reaction in me, I am a ghost walking among the dead. Some time ago I told you that I feared death; today I ask myself how I could have said such a thing if, after all, I was already *living* as a dead man. Can a dead person fear death? Only now do I begin to understand that I have nothing to die to, I only have to Be.

I have come to tell you of a dream I have had, as usual vivid and vibrating, so much so as not to be considered a dream.

I was on a street blocked by a house on fire. Slowly the flames expanded until they became a huge fire of a golden yellow colour, beautiful and completely transparent. The house collapsed and on the other side I could see your figure made of radiant fire, but of a different nature to the one in front of me.

Without hesitation I went into the fire and the ashes of the house. Suddenly I seemed to feel myself falling and the thing seemed strange because there was no precipice. When my fall ended I found myself beside you and you stretched your hand to me and then put your arm around my shoulders. As I wanted to realize how I could have managed to find myself suddenly with you and to see whether the flames were still burning, I tried to turn, but I was prevented from doing so by your arm around my shoulders.

Understanding my need, you told me: "Why are you looking at the ashes of your imcompleteness? The past has vanished completely, the future cannot be any longer because your *avidyā* seeds have been destroyed; you can do nothing but live the eternal present."

These words rang in my ears when I awoke. The event was so vivid and real that even when I opened my eyes I could still see the fire and feel myself burning. To distract myself I picked up a book at random, one of those you gave me; it was *The Way of Fire*. Many thoughts crowded my mind and many analogies came spontaneously to me. I left the book and entered into Silence of the mind.

I have told you about this experience; but do not speak to me of fire any more, I feel in flames still.

R. No, *my son*, I shall not speak to you of fire; I shall tell you only that in this dream life of mine the most beautiful event for me is to see the dawn. Today I have seen the dawn again, a beautiful dawn—and the dawn, we know, is the harbinger of the sure and happy message that the sun is reaching the Zenith.

INDEX

Absolute, 41, 52
-and relative 12-14, 15, 44
Acting, 111
Advaita Vedānta, 17-20, 23, 27, 31, 45, 55, 58, 61, 71-72, 83, 97, 109, 115, 117
Advaitin, 24, 25
Aparā Vidyā, 22
Aristotle, 59
Art of dying, 108
Asparśa yoga, 72
Asparśin, 33, 71
Asparśin Masters, 32
Ātman 97
Attachment, 66
Avidyā, 25, 44, 81

Becoming, 59, 91, 101
Being, 14, 24
Bhakta, 33
Birth, 48
Body, 114
Bradley, 63
Buddha, 108

Causal-germinal body, 102
Cause and effect, 28, 44-45
Christ, 108
Compensations, 88
—of the ego, 99-103
Conflict, 7
Constant, 12, 13-14, 39, 43-44, 47, 50, 52
Content, 91

Death, 65-69, 115, 118
Desire, 1, 100
Detachment, 82
Dialogue, viii, 2
Dimension (infra-sensorial), 19
Diogene Laertes, 60
Discrimination, 82
Dissatisfaction, 87
Dream experiences, 73, 75, 95, 106, 118-19

Dying to oneself, 104-10

Ego, 53, 56, 67-68, 81-82, 87-88, 106-09, 114, 117
Erudition, 82
Essence, 29
Esthetics, 71
Evolutionism, 51-53
Experience, 3
Experimentation, 117
Fanaticism, 56
Freedom, 7, 37, 58
Fulfilment, 77

Gauḍapāda, 31, 41-42, 56, 58
General and universal, 12, 18
Genius, 77

Happiness and bliss, 5
Harmony, 70-73
Heraclitus, 39
Identification, 1
Identity, 27
Ignorance, 69
Illusion, 38-39
Illusionism, 41
Impression (subconscious), 96
Infinite, 18
—and indefinite, 35
Īśvara, 20

Jīva, 36-37, 49-50, 95-97, 113-14
Jung and Western extroversion, 79-80

Kant, 13
Kierkegaard, 79
Knowledge, 13, 27-30, 63

Laws (of the universal and particular), 68, 69
Life, 15, 52-53
Līlā, 62
Logos, 60

Materialism, 84
Māyā, 22-24, 38, 39-50, 52-53, 66-67, 81-82, 91, 111
Melissos, 60
Memory, 86
Mind, 86-87, 90-91, 117
Monism, 23
Movement, 91-92
Mysteries (Great and Lesser), 21, 24

Necessity, 87
Nirguṇa Brahman, 21, 23-24, 34, 36-37, 47, 50, 112, 117
Non-being, 23
Non-dualism, 23, 25, 31, 41, 47
Non-duality, 21, 47

One, 18, 23, 29, 62
One-without-a-second, 38

Pantheism, 47
Parā Vidyā, 22
Parmenides, 39, 58-60
Patañjali, 31
Path of Fire, 58
Pax profunda, 102
Phenomenism, 42
Planck, Max, 13, 17, 41
Plato, 56, 61
Pleasure-pain, 107
Plotinus, 61, 62
Plutarch, 59
Point (geometrical, dimensionless), 35
Prakṛti, 48
Pralaya, 101
Puruṣa, 48
Pythagoras, 61

Qabbālāh, 57
Qualifications of the disciple, 75-78

Rāja-yogin, 33
Reality, 3, 5, 9-20, 22-27, 30, 38-39, 41-42, 53, 59, 63, 75, 78, 81-83, 88
Realization, 33, 82
Relative, 53

Sādhanā, 25, 71, 80, 81-84, 116
Saguṇa Brahman, 21, 23, 33, 84, 35-39, 48, 50
Śaṃkara, 21, 31, 41-44, 46, 51, 56, 58, 108, 111
Sensory life, 1
Socrates, 61
Spinoza, 62
Śruti, 21-22, 51
Stages of life (*āśrama*), 24
Subconsciousness, 115
Superimposition, 111
Supports, 114

Techniques, 105
Tertullianus, 79
Theism, 20
Time, 11
Timon, 60
Tradition, 56
Transmigration, 95-98
Truth, 2, 19-20
—and error, 24

Understanding, 31
Unity, 112-13
—of Tradition, 55-64
Upaniṣad, 117

Vigilance, 76
Vivekānanda, 66

Watchfulness, 105, 116

Yoga, 31-34
Yogin, 33, 77

Zero, metaphysical, 23